HISTORIC TULSA

An Illustrated History of Tulsa & Tulsa County

by Beryl Ford, Charles Ford, Rodger Randle, and Bob Burke

Foreword by William LaFortune

Commissioned by the Oklahoma Heritage Association and the Tulsa Historical Society

Oklahoma Horizons Series

Historical Publishing Network
A division of Lammert Incorporated
San Antonio, Texas

ISBN: 978-1-893619-59-1

Library of Congress Card Catalog Number: 2006927026

Historic Tulsa: An Illustrated History of Tulsa & Tulsa County

authors:	Bob Burke
	Beryl Ford
	Charles Ford
	Rodger Randle
editor:	Gini Moore Campbell
cover artist:	Wayne Cooper
contributing writers for "Sharing the Heritage":	Eric Dabney

Historical Publishing Network

president:	Ron Lammert
vice president:	Barry Black
project managers:	Wynn Buck
	Lou Ann Murphy
director of operations:	Charles A. Newton III
administration:	Angela Lake
	Donna M. Mata
	Judi Free
book sales:	Dee Steidle
production:	Colin Hart
	Craig Mitchell
	John Barr
	Evelyn Hart

Unless otherwise noted, photographs are from the Beryl Ford Rotary Club of Tulsa Collection.

The authors are indebted to Pam Hodges, Jerry Cornelius, Eric Dabney, Clayton Vaughn, Roxana Lorton, Linda Lynn, Mary Phillips, The Honorable Susan Savage, Royse and Sheila Parr, and the Rotary Club of Tulsa for assistance in preparing the manuscript and selecting photographs.

The book could not have been completed without the help of President Shannon Nance and Director of Publications and Education Gini Moore Campbell of the Oklahoma Heritage Association.

PRINTED IN KOREA.

CONTENTS

FOREWORD

BY WILLIAM LAFORTUNE

Tulsa County is unique in many ways—its geography, its culture, and its people. The county's history is rich and varied, with contributions from Native Americans, farmers and ranchers, oil men, industrialists, and modern philanthropists and public servants. Despite all differences in race, creed, financial status, or geographic residency—we are all Tulsa Countians—one big family.

For more than a century, the cities and towns of Tulsa County have joined hands to provide the very best service to residents of the county in areas of health, education, recreation, libraries, and law enforcement. Now we have embarked upon Vision 2025, one of the boldest and most visionary regional growth packages ever undertaken in the United States.

This is an exciting time in the life of Tulsa County. After Vision 2025 was approved by voters, we have seen mayors, city managers, city councilors, chambers of commerce, arts organizations, and neighborhood associations all united behind a single vision. We are celebrating the beginning of a new era for Tulsa County—not for ourselves but for future generations. Our vision for the future is for better jobs, more investment in our economic infrastructure, and emphasizing quality education and healthcare for our citizens.

The nation is noticing the vision of Tulsa County, a fact proven by Tulsa's selection as one of America's Most Livable Communities, a designation only presented every ten years. Vision 2025 also has gained Tulsa national recognition from the United States Conference of Mayors for outstanding management practices.

Vision 2025 is our greatest economic development tool. The future of Tulsa County depends on the revitalization and growth we will achieve with Vision projects. Putting cranes in the air will be a visible sign of progress and will create an environment of pride for our people.

Tulsa County is the greatest place in the world to live and work. We must build from past successes of cooperation among the cities and towns in the region to make our county even a greater place for our children and grandchildren.

William LaFortune, Mayor
City of Tulsa, 2002-2006

William "Bill" LaFortune was elected mayor of Tulsa in 2002. He previously served as an assistant attorney general for the State of Oklahoma, a Tulsa County special district judge, and Tulsa County district attorney.

✧

A ferry crossing on the Arkansas River near Eleventh Street in 1898. The ferry is carrying a chuckwagon and the foreman of a cattle herd being driven through the shallow river.

CHAPTER I

AN ANCIENT LAND

History runs deep in Tulsa County—from the earliest Native American inhabitants, to the cattlemen, the coming of the railroads, and the oil boom.

Tulsa County is old. Archaeologists may disagree on when humans first came to the area, but the evidence suggests that between 11,000 and 25,000 years ago people who hunted mammoth, camels, ground sloth, and other animals to extinction, visited the area that became Tulsa County. Because they used simple stone tools and worked with biodegradable materials such as wood and leather, there is little trace of their existence.

Several shallow seas covered prehistoric Tulsa which was ringed by subtropical forests and swamps. As the land became dry, lush grasslands attracted herds of animals that brought early hunters. To kill their prey, the Clovis Mammoth Hunters used a fluted projectile called a Clovis Point, one of which has been found along the Arkansas River near Tulsa. A forty-five-hundred-year-old petroglyph has been discovered on the ceiling of a cliff overhang just west of Tulsa.

Tulsa County was visited by two groups of prehistoric Native Americans—Plains Indians, who maintained a nomadic, hunter lifestyle, and Moundbuilders, who tended to live in permanent settlements and built an agricultural tradition around corn, beans, and squash.

The Moundbuilders of the Mississipian culture thrived in Oklahoma from A.D. 800 until 1200, when they suffered a severe decline. Historians are not certain whether changing climate, migration, disease, or invasion from Plains Indians eliminated 90 percent of the Mississippian culture. By the time Francisco Vasquez de Coronado explored the Southwest in 1540, the Plains culture was dominant in Oklahoma.

Both the Spanish and French claimed Tulsa County as part of their colonial empire. France ceded its claim to the area to Spain in 1763, regained control of the region in 1800, and then sold it as part of the Louisiana Purchase to the United States in 1803.

The tribes of the Wichita Confederation settled along the Arkansas River before being driven south by the more powerful Osage who had settled in Missouri in the early 1800s. The Osage hunted buffalo and built permanent villages. They were fierce warriors and defeated other tribes that fought for control of buffalo hunting lands in the new West.

In 1802, three thousand Osage relocated to land north of the Three Forks area of Oklahoma, where the Arkansas, Grand, and Verdigris Rivers meet. As conflict began between the Osage and other Native Americans, the federal government intervened. Treaties resulted in the Osage surrendering their claim to Tulsa County and other Oklahoma lands. That intervention allowed the movement of Creeks from Georgia and Alabama to what would become Indian Territory and later, eastern Oklahoma.

The Creek Nation was a confederacy, an alliance of independent tribes that became a single, dynamic institution. During the fourteenth century, the Creeks had claimed the Three Forks area of Oklahoma but had migrated southeastward, eventually settling in Alabama and Georgia where they built permanent and semi-permanent settlements, just like their Moundbuilder ancestors.

As whites began moving from the original colonies into the South, the federal government began to develop plans to move Native Americans to the wide open spaces of the West. The Lower Creeks, made up of mostly mixed-bloods, accepted removal from their ancient homeland and began moving to Oklahoma as early as 1825. However, the Upper Creeks, predominantly full-bloods, were opposed to removal and delayed their departure until forced to travel to Indian Territory along the infamous Trail of Tears in 1836-1837.

As pressure mounted for all Creeks to leave Georgia and Alabama, William McIntosh and Opothle Yahola became leaders of the pro-removal and anti-removal factions. McIntosh was a mixed blood who was educated by whites and tried to bridge the gap between his two peoples. Opothle Yahola advocated

✧

Oklahoma artist Charles Banks Wilson at work on his painting, Discovery and Exploration, *which depicts Vasquez de Coronado's travels across the Oklahoma Panhandle in 1541.*

separation of whites and Creeks and vehemently opposed any influence of white culture.

The first Lower Creeks arrived in Oklahoma in 1828. By 1830, the Creeks joined the Seminoles, Cherokees, Choctaws, and Chickasaws as the Five Civilized Tribes being relocated to Indian Territory. Because of decades of contact with Europeans and Americans, many Creeks spoke English and their literacy rates equaled those of white pioneers in Indian Territory. They built farm houses and laid out fields for their crops. In 1832, Washington Irving visited Broken Arrow, and wrote of "well stocked" farms and comfortable houses. Of the Creeks, Irving wrote, "They are a well made race, muscular and closely knit, with well formed thighs and legs. They have a gypsy fondness for brilliant colors and gay decorations, and are bright and fanciful objects when seen at a distance on the prairies."

By 1833 more than three hundred Creeks lived near present-day Broken Arrow. Two years earlier, a group of Creeks known as the Broken Arrow Creeks had traveled from Broken Arrow, Alabama, to settle in Indian Territory. By tradition, they carried coals from the campfire in their town in Alabama and rekindled it in their new home which took the name of Broken Arrow. Most of the Creeks began farming in the surrounding countryside.

The Upper Creeks were among the thousands who were marched westward by contractors employed by the federal government. On foot and by boat, the Creeks were herded like animals. By best estimates, less than half of the Creeks who left Alabama reached Indian Territory alive.

Members of the Creek community of Lochapoka in Alabama reached the Three Forks area in 1836 and decided to travel farther up the Arkansas River. When they came to a point just before the river made a great bend to the west, they stopped. On a small hill that rose from the river's sandy banks, Creek leader, Achee Yahola, and other tribal leaders gathered under a large oak tree. They laid out a square for their new home and solemnly scattered coals from a fire in their former town in Alabama that had been kept smoldering during their journey westward. As part of their spiritual tradition, flames from the coals rekindled, marking the link to the past and the beginning of a new existence on the frontier.

Lochapoka means "turtling" place in Creek, for the sea turtles that the Indians hunted in Alabama. Because there were no giant turtles in the Arkansas River, the Creeks did not attempt to name their village in Indian Territory for their village in Alabama. However, government engineers mapping the Creek Nation gave the village a name, Tallassee. The Lochapokas did not like the name and began calling their village, Tulsee Town. "Tul" is Creek for "town," causing Tulsee Town to be a redundancy.

WASHINGTON IRVING'S VISIT

In 1832, Washington Irving traveled into the wild lands beyond the frontier known to citizens of the young United States. He embarked on an expedition into the area west of Arkansas that had been reserved for emigrating Native Americans. His absorbing and descriptive account of his journey was first published in 1835 and soon became one of the first successful American travel books. Early in his trip, he encountered Osage Indians camped on the banks of the Arkansas River in present-day Tulsa County. Irving's description is the earliest written account of Tulsa County:

Our arrival created quite a sensation. A number of old men came forward and shook hands with us all severally; while the women and children huddled together in groups, staring at us wildly, chattering and laughing among themselves. We found that all the young men of the village had departed on a hunting expedition, leaving the women and children and old men behind…

Still hoping to reach the camp of the rangers before nightfall, we pushed on until twilight, when we were obliged to halt on the borders of a ravine. The rangers bivouacked under trees, at the bottom of the dell, while we pitched our tent on a rocky knoll near a running stream. The night came on dark and overcast, with flying clouds, and much appearance of rain. The fires of the rangers burnt brightly in the dell, and threw strong masses of light upon the robber-looking groups that were cooking, eating, and drinking around them.

To add to the wildness of the scene, several Osage Indians, visitors from the village we had passed, were mingled among the men. Three of them came and seated themselves by the fire. They watched everything that was going on around them in silence, and looked like figures of monumental bronze. We gave them food and, what they most relished, coffee; for the Indians partake in the universal fondness for this beverage, which pervades the West. Then they had made their supper, they stretched themselves, side by side, before the fire, and began a low nasal chant, drumming with their hands upon their breasts, by way of accompaniment. Their chant seemed to consist of regular staves, every one terminating, not in a melodious cadence, but in the abrupt interjection huh! uttered almost like a hiccup…

The beautiful forest in which we were encamped abounded in bee-trees; that is to say, trees in the decayed trunks of which wild bees had established their hives… At present the honey-bee swarms in myriads, in the noble groves and forests which skirt and intersect the prairies…It seems to me as if these beautiful regions answer literally to the description of the land of promise, "a land flowing with milk and honey," for the rich pasturage of the prairies is calculated to sustain herds of cattle as countless as the sands upon the seashore, while the flowers with which they are enameled render them a very paradise for the nectar-seeking bee.

✧

Washington Irving recorded his visit to an Osage village on the banks of the Arkansas River near present-day Tulsa in 1832 in his A Tour of the American Prairies. *This Wayne Cooper painting,* Washington Irving Meeting the Osage, *on display in the Oklahoma State Capitol, shows the Irving party camped for the night with the curious Osage mingling around the campfire, no doubt seeking a taste of coffee which intrigued even the Native American tribes of Oklahoma. A gift of Charles Ford, director of the Oklahoma State Senate Historical Preservation Fund, Inc.*

The oak under which the ceremony occurred became known as the Creek Council Oak and still stands stately between Seventeenth and Eighteenth Streets and Cheyenne and Denver Avenues in Tulsa. Acorns from this tree were cultivated by the Tulsa Parks Department and planted in various locations around the city during Tulsa's centennial celebration.

Achee Yahola built a cabin on newly cleared land as his followers established farms within a reasonable distance of the new community. Very few whites entered the area and life was peaceful.

From the mid-1840s through the Civil War, Native Americans, with the help of a few white missionaries who had established missions among the Creeks, advanced civilization in what would become Tulsa County. Presbyterian missionary Robert M. Loughridge built the White Church, the first church building in Tulsa County, in Broken Arrow in the 1840s. Within a decade, the Methodists and Baptists had a presence in Broken Arrow. The churches provided education for local families.

In 1848, a Creek rancher, Lewis Perryman, and five sons moved their ranching operation from the Big Spring community on the Verdigris River to the Lochapoka square and built a mansion, including slaves quarters. The Perrymans were mixed-bloods who had voluntarily settled in the Three Forks area in the 1820s. Lewis Perryman, an Upper Creek, had arrived with his four wives in 1828. The family's ranch included the area between Twenty-first Street on the north and Seventy-first Street on the south, between the Arkansas River on the west and present-day Broken Arrow on the east. Many members of the family were converted at churches established by missionaries. James Perryman became pastor of the White Church at Broken Arrow.

Then came the Civil War. Most Creeks allied with the Confederacy. But Opothle Yahola sided with the Union and gathered more than

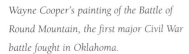

Wayne Cooper's painting of the Battle of Round Mountain, the first major Civil War battle fought in Oklahoma.

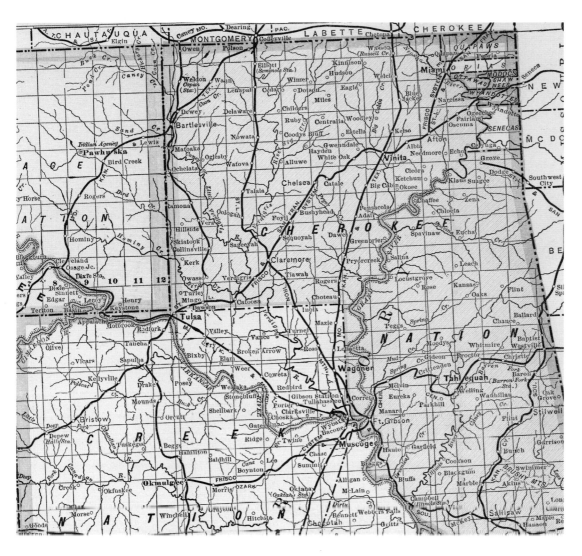

seven thousand men, women, and children for the trek to safety in Kansas. However, the refugees were attacked near present Keystone on November 19, 1861, in what has become known as the Battle of Round Mountain. Texas cavalry and Confederate Indians commanded by Colonel Douglas H. Cooper ran the refugees across the Arkansas River, through present Sand Springs, and into Tallassee. The Lochapokas fed the retreating refugees and joined the exodus to Kansas.

On the day after Christmas, better armed Texas and Arkansas Confederate forces overcame Opothle Yahola's band at Hominy Creek. Many Creeks died. Some of those who lived escaped north to Kansas—but hundreds of prisoners were rounded up and taken back to a sandbar on the Arkansas near Tallassee, and executed.

Somehow, the Lochapoka people survived and were allowed to return to their community after the Civil War. Even though their peace

was guaranteed by the federal government, their economy and town were destroyed. Rather than rebuild in a cluster on the original site, the people built cabins in the surrounding area. The Perrymans and other families reestablished their lives. George Perryman married a full-blood woman of the Lochapoka community and built a new home, the "White House" at what is today Thirty-eighth Street and Trenton Avenue, from lumber brought by wagon from Coffeyville, Kansas.

For several years, George Perryman's brother, Josiah, informally delivered mail to the nine hundred residents of Tulsee Town. For his mail distribution center, he used a log cabin that stood at present-day Thirty-first Street and Trenton Avenue. In March, 1879, a room added onto his brother's home was designated as the place for the first post office to serve what became Tulsa. The government shortened the traditional Tulsee Town to Tulsa.

✧

In the northwest section of present-day Tulsa is a point where boundaries of three Indian nations met—the Osage, Cherokee, and Creek.

The first Tulsa post office was not a busy place. Sometimes, only one letter per week was received or posted. The incoming mail was stamped with an official government seal that read, "Tulsa, I.T." Josiah Perryman's annual salary as Tulsa postmaster was $15.

Throughout the 1870s, a significant number of whites settled among the Creeks in Tulsa County. In 1874, William P. Moore, by virtue of having a federal trader's license, established a store at Broken Arrow.

In 1880, the Atlantic and Pacific Railroad won the right to lay railroad tracks into Indian Territory. After Atlantic and Pacific declared bankruptcy, its successor, the St. Louis and San Francisco (Frisco) Railroad extended the tracks in 1882 from Vinita south to the Arkansas River. Railroad crews camped near the river at the site of present downtown Tulsa. The new destination of the Frisco was dubbed Tulsa to honor the Creeks who had first settled there.

Two brothers from Tennessee, Harry C. and James Monroe Hall, were supervisors on the

construction crew that laid out a town site for Tulsa. The new town needed a Main Street on which to place stores and a stable. Main Street and the surrounding streets were platted perpendicular to the railroad tracks, creating streets in the downtown area that do not run true east-west or north-south.

When the tracks reached the new site on August 7, 1882, a tent city awaited workers. The only permanent dwelling in Tulsa was Noah Partridge's cabin. All other businesses and dwellings were made of canvas. As business increased, tents gave way to shoddily constructed frame buildings. The first such

✧

Left: The first residence built in Tulsa, Indian Territory, was constructed by Jack Burgess. The house was located in what later was the 500 block of North Cincinnati Avenue.

Below: James Monroe Hall's general merchandise store in 1896. Hall was a shrewd businessman who knew how to advertise his low prices.

Top: The Lynch Brothers store opened for business in 1893 on the northeast corner of what is now First Street and Main Street.

Middle: The Reverend George Mowbray (second from left) was pastor of the First Methodist Episcopal Church and preached to Indians in the countryside. He took a course in embalming in 1890 and became Tulsa's undertaker. He later was mayor of Tulsa from 1902 to 1904 and conducted the town's first census.

Bottom: Thomas Jefferson Archer operated this general store on Main Street after his first building, built in 1883, was destroyed by fire.

business was Jeff Archer's general store.
Soon false-front buildings housed stores
owned by the Perryman brothers. It would be
more than a decade until Tulsa had its first
masonry building.

The Halls opened a commissary to provide
food and supplies for new residents who
arrived weekly. Harry Hall became known as
the founder of Tulsa—his brother, J. M.,
became known as the father of Tulsa.

Chauncey Owen opened Tulsa's first hotel,
Tulsa House, with twenty-two rooms. Later

owners renamed the hotel St. Elmo. The
Presbyterians won the honor of having Tulsa's
first formal church, First Presbyterian Church,
established on October 5, 1885.

From its first day, Tulsa became known
as the heart of cow country. The railroad
allowed ranchers to ship their cattle to
market. Huge ranches sprang up to Tulsa's
east and south—Daniel Childers at Broken
Arrow, Clement Rogers along the Verdigris
River, Green Yeargin at Sperry, and A. W.
Hoots at Skiatook.

CHAPTER II

BLACK GOLD

Tulsa's first traffic jams were caused by cattle. Herds literally took over the streets when cattlemen arrived. Historian Fannie Misch described the scene, "Train load after train load of cattle were unloaded at the town stockyards…and the uproar of milling longhorns and yelling cowboys disturbed people for days as the cattle were spread out fanwise for the Osage Pasture or the Big Pasture southeast."

Early day merchants were glad for the influx of business that the proliferation of cattle herds brought. However, the rowdiness had a downside. Misch wrote, "When ranch paydays arrived and the range riders galloped their ponies up Main Street shooting out lighted windows, the settlers quickly learned to close the stores, blow out the lamps, and lie on the floor. Even the train depot remained closed!"

Tulsa was incorporated on January 18, 1898, and remained a cow town until oil was discovered shortly after the turn of the twentieth century. For 30 years, oil men had been looking for oil in Oklahoma. Early settlers reported natural oil seeps south and west of Tulsa near Sapulpa, Red Fork, and Glenn Pool. However, it was a well drilled near Red Fork, on an allotment assigned to Creek citizen Sue Davis Bland that changed Tulsa forever.

On June 24, 1901, just before midnight, the drilling bit ruptured a pocket of gas at slightly more than five hundred feet in the well. Oil gushed from the ground, causing the word to spread far and wide. Tulsa leaders were behind getting out the word, because they wanted to control all activity in their trade territory. Newspapers from Oklahoma to Kansas City carried bold headlines that Red Fork had risen from its ranks as a tiny Creek town on the west side of the Arkansas River to an oil boom town.

Red Fork was considerably smaller than Tulsa when the Sue Bland No. 1 was brought in, but the new boom town was growing daily. Even though would-be oil men descended upon the town in great numbers, the gusher slowed to a trickle and other wells around Red Fork were never great producers. However, citizens of Red Fork and Tulsa had a taste of what oil could do to transform a town and its people.

The Arkansas River separated Red Fork and Tulsa. The only access between the two towns was the Frisco Railroad bridge. A ride across the river on a train cost sixteen cents. Tulsa businessmen were concerned that Red Fork would become a center of trade, taking money from Tulsa's economy. A bond issue to build a bridge across the river failed, but three young businessmen— George T. Williamson, J. D. Haler, and M. L. Baird—agreed to finance the bridge privately.

There were no technical problems, only bureaucratic difficulties, in building a bridge across the Arkansas. Before beginning the project, Williamson, Haler, and Baird had to get permission from local Indian leaders and from government officials all the way to Washington, D.C. When confronted with the roadblock of not allowing another bridge over what was classified as a navigable stream, the three entrepreneurs promised the government that if the Arkansas River ever became navigable at that location, they would bear the expense of making the bridge a drawbridge.

The three bridge-builders-to-be ignored reports that the river bottom would not support a bridge. They built a coffer dam to hold back the water until sand could be removed. Then, they used old boilers for forms, and filled them with concrete. The piers reached into the river bottom to a solid stratum of limestone. At a cost of $50,000, the toll bridge was completed on January 4, 1904. Signs at the bridge's tollgate read, "You said we couldn't do it, but we did."

Tulsans built hotels and restaurants to service workers from the Red Fork field. A special train, "Coal Oil Johnny," transported workers in the morning to their jobs in the oil patch, and returned them to eat and sleep in Tulsa each night.

❖

Early Tulsa was truly a cow town. Thousands of cattle were driven through downtown streets, cutting deep ruts into the thoroughfares, and trampling residents' vegetable gardens.

Top: An 1897 street scene in Dawson, a community now within the city limits of Tulsa. Named for its first postmaster, Wilbur A. Dawson, Dawson had its own post office from 1895 to 1949.

Middle: The Katy Railroad Depot in the early 1900s was located in the 400 block of North Main Street. The coming of the railroad was a key event in the birth and growth of Tulsa.

Bottom: The Tulsa skyline, looking south from Standpipe Hill on North Cincinnati Avenue in 1903.

The real oil boom in Tulsa County began on November 22, 1905, when Robert Galbreath and Frank Chesley brought in a true gusher on a farm owned by Ida Berryhill Glenn about ten miles south of Tulsa. Four months later, another gusher began flowing. Wells sprang up in a field that eventually extended eight miles. Within two years, more than 1,000 wells had been drilled and nearly 100 oil companies operated within the Glenn Pool, appropriately labeled in the infant oil industry as "the Richest Little Oil Field in the World."

Tulsa was at the center of the oil boom, even though the discovery of oil was in adjacent towns. That was by design, because Tulsa business leaders were shrewd in recognizing that Tulsa, with its service by five railroads, would become the commercial center to supply the oilfields.

Within a short time, worldwide publicity brought thousands of new people to Tulsa. Housing was so scarce that men slept on derrick floors. Tanks could not be built fast enough to store the oil that the Glenn Pool field produced. Oil was dumped into earthen storage pits, a cheap and easy way to store excess crude. Huge lakes of oil attracted thousands of wild birds that died after landing in

Top, left: The Sue Bland No. 1 was the first successful oil well in Tulsa County. The strike brought wide publicity for Tulsa and triggered oil fever in Oklahoma.

Top, right: As a leader among the small group of pioneers in the village of Tulsa, Jay Forsythe was most influential in starting the schools, the first bank, and building the cultural future of the city. After arduous years on the western frontier and along historic cattle trails, he came to Tulsa in 1892 where he spent the next 42 years as a businessman, real estate developer and city official. His son-in-law, Robert Turner Epperson, founded the first Tulsa opera house known as the Epperson Opera House.

Below: Oklahoma's petroleum heritage is commemorated by a huge mural, "Oklahoma Black Gold," that appears in the State Capitol.

COURTESY OF THE OKLAHOMA ARTS COUNCIL.

✧

Top: Looking west on Third Street across Main Street in Tulsa in 1909.

Above: Wooden derricks rushed into the sky every three hundred feet in the Glenn Pool oil field. The first well was brought in November 22, 1905, signaling unprecedented growth in the oil industry in Tulsa County.

Right: Gushers were regular sights as oil wells were drilled with frenzy in the Glenn Pool.

the crude. After evaporation, the area turned into a tar pit.

At first, wooden storage tanks were built, but they leaked badly and were notorious for catching on fire from lightning strikes. Huge plumes of smoke over vast tank farms were not an uncommon sight. Even after wooden tanks were replaced by steel structures, tank fires continued. Refinery workers often extinguished fires by using Civil War cannons, firing solid shot to pierce the tanks below the flames. The non-burning oil ran out of the tank into a surrounding dike. When the tank was empty, the fire burned itself out.

The Glenn Pool discovery was significant for Tulsa County's economy. Not only did the strike confirm the fortunes of newcomers, the $28 million spent on developing the field made a huge ripple in the local economy. Historian Danney Goble wrote, "It was spent as capital with drilling companies, freight companies, and supply companies. It was spent as wages in Tulsa's stores and for Tulsa homes. It was spent on necessities, on luxuries, on children—and on gambling, liquor, and women. It made Tulsa rich. It made Tulsa wild. And it made Tulsa big."

As early as 1904, Tulsa businessmen formally organized efforts to promote the town and attract more business. Booster trains, complete with bands and celebrities, traveled east to convince settlers to come to Tulsa. In 1908 a Frisco booster train carried 100 Tulsans on a 19-city tour. In Chicago, the booster band stopped trading on the Board of Trade. When worried investors in New York City asked what happened, the reply was "Tulsa has the floor."

In 1906 the Bird Creek Oil Field was opened in north Tulsa and, within months, claimed more than one thousand producing wells. New businesses related to the oil fields opened. Passenger and freight rail traffic greatly increased.

Almost overnight, Tulsa graduated from being a boomtown to a powerful and proud city. Throngs of laborers built tank farms to store the glut of oil that was being pumped from wells within dozens of miles of Tulsa. The first tank farm was built in west Tulsa for the Texas Company, better known as Texaco. Standard

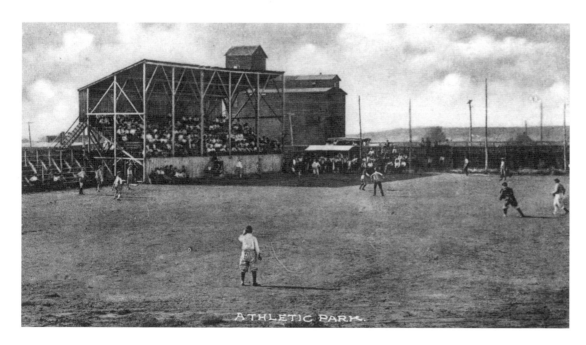

Top: Tulsa's Main Street in 1905. When it rained, wagons were mired in the mud up to their axles.

Middle: The Hotel Alcorn was Tulsa's premiere hotel in 1905. The building was a remodeled stable.

Bottom: Baseball was a popular sport in Tulsa by 1905 when this photograph was taken at the Tulsa Athletic Park, located between First and Second Streets just west of the Midland Valley Railroad. The same year, professional baseball came to Tulsa when businessman Billy Rupp fielded a team he called the "Oilers."

Above: In 1905, Tulsa's first high school building was built on the site of the former Presbyterian Mission School at Fourth Street and Boston Avenue.

Bottom, left: The Hotel Robinson was located on the southwest corner of Third and Main Streets, built in 1905 after the oil strike at Glenn Pool.

Bottom, right: The Hotel Brady was built to accommodate the influx of oil men. More oil deals were struck in the lobbies of Tulsa's hotels than in the oilfields.

Oil, managed as part of John D. Rockefellers' worldwide empire, built a pipe line that connected Tulsa with its refinery in Louisiana. By April, 1907, the line carried twenty thousand barrels of Oklahoma crude each day.

When Oklahoma became the forty-sixth state of the Union on November 16, 1907, Tulsa was easily the logical choice to be chosen as the seat of Tulsa County. The city had outgrown other cities in the county consistently in every population count and was not only the center of commerce for the county, but a large segment of Oklahoma.

However, delegates to the constitutional convention had great difficulty in shaping a county of which Tulsa would be the county seat. The Enabling Act which allowed the creation of Oklahoma prevented map makers from including any Osage territory in Tulsa County. Therefore, it was not possible to create a square county. Rogers County delegates were successful in placing Collinsville in Rogers County, a move

that was an embarrassment to delegates from Tulsa County.

With the help of Muskogee County delegate, and Oklahoma's first governor, Charles N. Haskell, the present boundary

lines of Tulsa County were drawn, except for one-half of Collinsville that was annexed to Tulsa County in 1918. At the constitutional convention in Guthrie, Tulsan Flowers Nelson worked tirelessly to include Dawson and Owasso in Tulsa County, over objections of Rogers County delegates.

In 1908, newspaperman Patrick C. Doyle moved his printing press from Pennsylvania, the heart of America's first oil strike, to Tulsa and changed his newspaper's name to the Oil and Gas Journal. With the industry's "bible" locating in Tulsa, other oil field suppliers and investors followed. John D. Rockefeller ordered his Prairie Oil and Gas Company to establish headquarters in the new Commercial National Bank Building in Tulsa. The Texas Company soon took over space in the new Mayo Building from which to conduct its Tulsa area operations.

In 1912 the Cushing Field was opened just west of Tulsa and quickly became the tenth largest oil field in the United States in the first half of the twentieth century. Within a few years, the Cushing Field produced one-sixth of the oil marketed in America.

Tulsa became the transport, refining, and financial center for the development of the nation's huge oil strike, all within a hundred miles of the once sleepy Creek village. The activity gave rise to the claim that Tulsa was the "Oil Capital of the World." Strangely, no one seriously questioned the statement. Oil transformed Tulsee Town from a frontier hamlet into a modern, bustling urban environment. Boston Avenue in

✧

Top, left: The 1903 construction of a steel toll bridge to carry pedestrians and wagons across the Arkansas River near Eleventh Street allowed Tulsa access to the Red Fork and Glenn Pool oilfields. The bridge opened in January 1904.

Above: Lon Lewis was Tulsa County's first sheriff.

Left: As Tulsa grew, telephone service was established by the Pioneer Telephone Company. Lineman Joe Hill was later electrocuted in the line of duty.

Top: In March, 1905, members of Tulsa's business community organized a promotional trip to Terre Haute, Indiana, to convince people in Indiana that Tulsa was the place to live and work. In the front row, second from the right, is Will Rogers, known then as "Bill Rogers," who accompanied the Tulsans to entertain audiences with his rope tricks and humor.

Middle: The Frisco Railroad Depot on July 3, 1908. The depot was located where Boston Avenue crossed the Frisco tracks.

Bottom: Tulsa County citizens were proud of their country and hosted huge celebrations each Fourth of July.

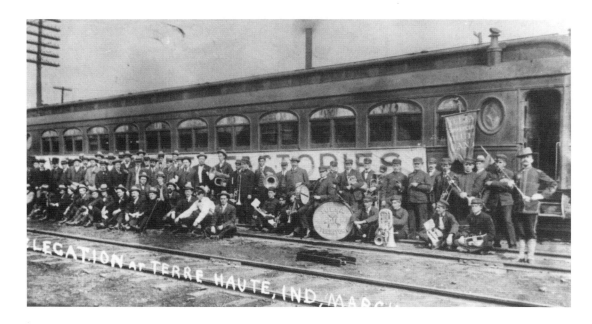

Top: Paving of Tulsa's city streets began in earnest in 1907. All men over 18 and under 45 were required to give one day's work to the project or pay a $3 tax.

Middle: One of the bands in Tulsa played at the Republican State Convention in 1907.

Bottom: Looking north on Main Street from Second Street in 1893. Dr. Sam Kennedy is on the porch with his leg over the railing.

downtown Tulsa became one of America's busiest streets.

As Tulsa grew, leaders looked for ways to provide an adequate water supply. The Arkansas River was unusable for drinking water, and even bathing. Many residents relied on bottled water or wells. Beginning in 1911, when he arrived as editor of the Tulsa World, Eugene Lorton began writing frequent editorials about the need for a good water supply. In 1915 he presented the idea for Tulsa to get its water from Spavinaw Creek, sixty-five miles to the northeast.

At first, Lorton's idea was dismissed as too expensive and senseless. However, after a few hundred more editorials, and citizens continuing to suffer through horrible tasting and horrible looking water, voters approved a $6.8 million bond issue and brought water from Spavinaw Creek. With an abundant water supply for both residential and commercial use, Tulsa continued its unprecedented growth.

Huge fortunes were made in early Tulsa by entrepreneurs whose name have become synonymous with the oil and gas industry. Harry Sinclair, a native of West Virginia, began providing wood for derricks. Soon, he swapped for leases and built small oil companies into a vast fortune. He made so much money, he brought his brother, Earl, into the business.

Two Texas cousins, Robert McFarlin and James Chapman, heard about the oil strike and moved to Tulsa. By the time of the Cushing Field strike, their McMan Oil Company was the world's largest independent oil company.

William Grove "Bill" Skelly grew up in the Pennsylvania oil fields. Skelly, who formed Skelly Oil Company, an innovator in oil field

technology, moved to Tulsa in 1912 and set up offices in the Hotel Tulsa, where billions of dollars of oil deals were consummated. Legend has it that Harry Sinclair formed the Sinclair-White Oil Company after a poker game in the hotel. Another confirmed story is of oil man Josh Cosden writing a $12 million check to close a deal in the lobby of the Hotel Tulsa.

Danney Goble wrote about the Hotel Tulsa, "At one time or another, everybody who was anybody in oil passed through that lobby, making deals, swapping information, hustling business, and hustling each other. On a typical evening, one might see Tom Slick, Bill Skelly, and one or both of the Sinclairs trading jokes beside one of its marble-clad pillars. Cosden, McFarlin, and Chapman might be huddled around another, whispering quietly while some newcomer lounged purposefully nearby, hoping to pick up some information he could use."

J. Paul Getty made Tulsa home and founded Getty Oil Company. Getty was labeled "the richest man in the world" at one time. Getty's

Right: Built in 1919, the Sinclair Building at Fifth and Main Streets was the headquarters for the billion-dollar oil company founded by Harry F. Sinclair.

Below: Oklahoma's first automobile manufacturing plant opened in 1912. The Tulsa Automobile Corporation, with T. J. Hartman as president, built a car called the "Tulsa Four," because of its four-cylinder engine. In 1913, one of the cars finished ninth in the Indianapolis 500 auto race. The Tulsa Four was equipped with artillery-type wood wheels and eleven-inch fenders to protect the body. An advertisement boasted, "Note the graceful sweep of the full stream-line body with double cowl and sloping louvered hood…Unusual leg room in the front seat and roomy comfort in the rear is apparent…The air of sturdiness and burly power is unmistakable." The Tulsa Chamber of Commerce bought a touring model of the Tulsa Four. A plant fire in 1919 hampered the struggling company which folded after the 1923 model was produced.

father, George Getty, was an early-day oil man who formed a partnership with his son. From a $6-per-week room at the Cordova Hotel in Tulsa, young Getty scouted surrounding areas for oil leases.

Tulsa-based Cities Service Oil Company initiated the first large-scale geological survey in the search for oil and gas. Within a few years after Charles Gould became the company's first geologist, there were as many as 250 geologists on the payroll.

Tulsa County was full of rich people. The Tulsa Chamber of Commerce claimed to have fifty millionaires on its finance committee. Many oil companies had their own buildings, which resulted in the evolution of Tulsa's landscape.

By the early 1920s, Tulsa's telephone book contained listings for more than 400 oil and gas companies, far more than the combined number of grocery stores, doctors, and lawyers. In 1921, 16 oil companies employed nearly 17,000 Tulsans, half the labor force.

GHOST OFFICES

Tulsa County had many more post offices in the past than now exist. From 1884 to 1917, the main post office was moved from one side of Main Street to the other, from First Street to Fourth Street, every time a new postmaster was appointed. Finally, in 1917, the government constructed a post office building on the northwest corner of West Third Street and Boulder Avenue. In 1967, the post office moved to its present location at Fourth Street and Denver Avenue.

The Frisco Railroad was responsible for the establishment of many post offices that have since been eliminated. The railroad's policy was to build a side track every four to six miles to make it easier to load cattle for shipment. Often, villages sprang up at the cattle loading sidings.

Red Fork was established in 1883. A post office served residents of the area from January 3, 1884, to July 31, 1928.

On October 4, 1907, a post office was established at West Eighteenth Street and the Frisco track in West Tulsa, a settlement that began in the 1880s and grew rapidly after the Glenn Pool oil discovery and the construction of the Cosden and Uncle Sam Refinery on the west bank of the Arkansas River. In 1909 the area was annexed to the city of Tulsa and the post office became the West Tulsa station of the main Tulsa post office on December 31, 1917.

A post office was opened in the community of Carbondale on January 27, 1927, for residents who lived in the area around West Forty-seventh Street and West Thirtieth Avenue. The village was named after a town in southern Illinois and was planned as a large industrial complex. Shares were sold to finance a carbon black manufacturing plant, but the plant burned before beginning operation. The post office closed after Carbondale was annexed to the city of Tulsa in 1928.

A coal and cattle-loading side track was located by the Frisco just west of present Sheridan Avenue and the railroad track. In 1885, thousands of tons of coal were strip-mined in the area by teams of mules and scrapers. The coal mining settlement was named after coal miner Wilbur A. Dawson. Dawson was designated as an official post office from February 28, 1895, to October 31, 1949, when the area was annexed by the city of Tulsa. After coal production was phased out, aviation made Dawson a roaring community.

Alsuma, a community on the Missouri-Kansas-Texas Railroad (MKT) six miles east of Tulsa, was first called "Welcome" because blacks were welcome there. In 1906 the name was changed to Alsuma. Its post office was open from May 17, 1905, to June 15, 1906. The area, located near East Forty-sixth Street and Mingo Road, was annexed by the city of Tulsa on April 15, 1966.

Scales had a post office from June 10, 1904, to March 31, 1909. It was a coal mining "shack town" named for coal mine operator Henry Scales. The town, populated by seventy families, was located along the Frisco Railroad.

Mohawk was a tiny community located on the Santa Fe Railroad one-half mile east of North Harvard Avenue. Named for the Mohawk Indians, the village had a post office from May 18, 1906, to July 10, 1915.

Rockspur served a village that grew up around a side track near a rock quarry where the Frisco crossed North Harvard Avenue. Rockspur had an official post office from June 21, 1901, to June 30, 1902. Quarry workmen and local farmers and ranchers were served by a trading post on a wagon road from Tulsa to Dawson.

Poag was a community that never had a post office. It was located east of the intersection of U.S. 75 and Oklahoma 117 on the west side of Polecat Creek on the Midland Valley Railroad right-of-way. Poag was a crude oil field camp occupied by workers who serviced nearby wells.

Another Tulsa County ghost town is Watkins, one and a half miles north of Glenpool on the bank of Coal Creek. It was the site of the Gulf Oil Company's railroad loading docks on the Midland Valley Railroad's spur line serving the Glenn Pool oil field.

CHAPTER III

PICKING UP THE PIECES

World War I had a major impact on Tulsa. Thousands of Tulsans answered the call of their country and volunteered to fight in the war in Europe. Tulsans formed an ambulance company in the Army's Forty-Second Division and students from Kendall College, now the University of Tulsa, formed Company D, Second Battalion of the 111th Army Engineers.

Oil became the lifeblood of the Allies effort in winning World War I. One Allied leader said, "The Allies floated to victory on a sea of oil." The increased demand for oil caused prices to shoot from 40 cents a barrel to $2.25 a barrel by the end of the conflict. Production in the fields around Tulsa increased accordingly, reaching 180 million barrels per year by 1918. Oklahoma supplied one-third of the nation's oil during World War I.

Tulsans who did not leave to fight did their part at home. Under the guidance of Chamber of Commerce President Robert McFarland and bankers Newton Graham and J. M. Berry, five Liberty Loan bond campaigns raised more than $32 million in Tulsa County for the war effort.

After World War I, black immigrants from surrounding states continued to be drawn to the Greenwood District of north Tulsa, named for Greenwood, Arkansas, the home of the Patton brothers who made Tulsa's first survey. Tulsa's black population increased from 1,429 at statehood to 8,803 in 1919, making Greenwood larger than most Oklahoma towns. The area was served by businesses in modern buildings and Greenwood's citizens enjoyed a reasonably good life with handsome churches and schools.

Tulsa, and America, lived double lives in 1921. Schools for whites and blacks were separate, but certainly not equal. Black teachers earned slightly more than half of that of a white teacher. A large police force patrolled south Tulsa, but only one officer was assigned to Greenwood, and he could not arrest a white person. A city ordinance prevented blacks from moving into all white neighborhoods. Tulsa was a segregated city.

On May 30, 1921, a fateful event occurred in an elevator at Renberg's, a fashionable clothing store located in the Drexel Building on South Main Street. Dick Rowland, a black young man, stepped onto the elevator that was occupied by a 17-year-old white girl, Sarah Page. No one except Rowland and Page really know what happened, but the girl ran screaming from the elevator, claiming she had been assaulted. Rowland said he had stumbled and bumped into the girl.

The following day, Rowland was arrested and rumors circulated that he would be lynched for the crime. Up to 100 black men gathered around the county jail to prevent a lynching. When a large group of whites arrived, the air was tense. It began with frightened talk—then at least one shot rang out.

During the night, armed gangs of angry whites invaded the Greenwood district and took guns and ammunition from sixteen pawn shops and hardware stores. Black resistance was ineffective to stop the rampage as mobs shot, robbed, and burned their way through the Greenwood District. Oklahoma Governor J. B. A. Robertson declared martial law. National Guard troops arrived the following morning to help restore order. However, the damage had been done.

Thirty five blocks of Greenwood had been looted or burned. More than eleven hundred black families were homeless. Six thousand blacks were rounded up by special deputies appointed by Tulsa Mayor T. D. Evans and placed in holding areas. In the first 24 hours after the National Guard arrived, more than 200 black and white citizens required surgery. The Red Cross rendered medical assistance to another 531.

The reporting of the 1921 Tulsa race riot is the most controversial single event among historians in Oklahoma. Estimates of those killed in the riot range from 36 to 300. The *New York Times* reported, "The entire black belt of Tulsa is now only a smoldering heap of blacked ruins. Hardly a negro shanty

✧

Black smoke covered the Greenwood District in north Tulsa on June 1, 1921, as thirty-five blocks of the all-black neighborhood were looted or burned.

is standing…State guardsmen with fixed bayonets patrol all the streets…. Domestic animals wandering among the wreckage give the only token of life over a desolate territory."

Tulsa leaders had much to be proud of from the time of the birth of the city through 1921. But the label of Tulsa as the scene of one of America's most devastating race riots was not what boosters wanted to see in newsprint. It was the city's darkest hour, and leaders met in groups to see how to control the damage and somehow try to mend fences with the people of Greenwood. Tulsans turned down offers from outside agencies to rebuild the black district.

Sadly, the official investigation of the riot showed that deep discrimination still existed.

A grand jury found that the presence of armed blacks was the direct cause of the riot. In the end, only one man, a black man, served any time for the crimes committed during the dark days. Garfield Thompson was convicted of carrying a concealed weapon and served 30 days in the county jail. Prosecutors failed to pursue criminal charges against anyone else.

The riot had an ugly result—thousands of Tulsans joined the Ku Klux Klan, bands of mostly middle-class workers who believed law enforcement officials had failed to clean up problems associated with gambling and prostitution. After a Klan whipping squad rendered its own justice to an alleged dope peddler, Governor Jack Walton declared war on the Klan and declared martial law in Tulsa, for the second time in two years. Military forces set up headquarters in the Hotel Tulsa and suspended operations of the city and county government. When the *Tulsa Tribune* printed an editorial calling for an end to martial law, the National Guard closed down the newspaper.

Governor Walton authorized a military tribunal to accept testimony regarding the Klan and alleged lawlessness in Tulsa. Over a period of several weeks, armed soldiers patrolled the streets while information was collected on 220 incidents in the county. The huge bound book that documented the tribunal's actions shows that only four of the incidents were race related—the remainder was complaints about moral and physical

terrorism. Only 4 of 31 Klansmen who were indicted were punished.

Even though there was no official apology for the Tulsa riot, Eugene Lorton, publisher of the *Tulsa World*, apologized in a front page editorial and started a relief fund with his own money. Lorton strongly condemned the actions of the Klan and warned that the organization that had been established to save the country from an imaginary peril had become the "very greatest peril the republic faces."

Nature also dealt Tulsa a body blow in the 1920s. In June, 1923, the Arkansas River left its banks. Flood waters left four thousand Tulsans homeless—refineries and businesses were flooded. All roads into the city except from the north were closed. Anyone traveling from Tulsa to Sand Springs had to do so by boat.

Local leaders began the International Petroleum Exposition (IPE), a gathering of the exclusive worldwide fraternity of oil and gas explorers and developers that same year. The

IPE was the premier annual event in the petroleum industry and was billed as the largest gathering of international oil men in the world. The exposition offered oil-related businesses the opportunity to tout their products to the leading companies in the industry.

By 1927, Tulsa was home to fifteen hundred oil-related companies whose operations in the mid-continent fields produced two-thirds of the nation's oil. Tulsa had no resemblance to Tulsee Town.

Even though the 1920s was a time of natural and human disaster, it was a decade of extraordinary prosperity in Tulsa County. Even after the stock market crash in 1929, signaling the onset of the greatest and deepest economic downturn in modern history, Tulsa was insulated—at least for awhile. The oil industry was one of the last to be affected by the Great Depression.

While the economy was still strong, cultural development continued in Tulsa. The opera house, that had been completed in 1906 even before the construction of sewers, paved streets, and sidewalks, signaled Tulsa's appreciation for the arts.

The Great Depression wove its destructive forces throughout the land, By the winter of 1931, soup lines were commonplace in Tulsa as banks closed, factories shut their doors, and

hungry families, desperate for work, camped on the steps of the county courthouse.

By 1932, 7,000 Tulsans were out of work and welcomed the election of Franklin D. Roosevelt as president. One of Roosevelt's actions was to push through Congress the creation of the Works Progress Administration (WPA), admittedly a make-work program, part of Roosevelt's New Deal. More than two dozen WPA projects in Tulsa County provided the area with major improvements, including the Tulsa Rose Garden and a new reservoir at Mohawk Park. Unemployed Tulsa County citizens built sidewalks, benches, parks, stadiums, and even compiled the first documented history of the city.

Oil prices plunged during the Great Depression, causing havoc among Tulsa's oil companies. With the help of the federal and state governments, oil prices stabilized by 1934, reaching and passing the dollar-a-barrel

mark again. A practical effect of the Depression was that Tulsa County's once independent oil barons had to admit that government regulation had saved their fortunes.

Labor strife hit Tulsa County hard in 1938. West Tulsa refinery workers struck the Mid-Continent Petroleum Corporation's plant. The strike made national headlines for more than a year as national guardsmen protected the refinery with bayonets, machine guns, and barbed-wire barriers.

The city's pioneers and churches worked hard to provide for the less fortunate in Tulsa County. In the shadow of huge mansions, on the fringe of Tulsa, were tent cities, home to poorer families who had been attracted to the oil capital. Churches took the lead in trying to solve the county's social problems, raising huge sums of money to finance YMCA and public health projects. Free health clinics were in place in Tulsa County prior to the Great Depression.

✧

Above: Tulsa's earliest motel was the Pierce Pennant Terminal at 12200 East Eleventh Street, on the famous Route 66. The "Mother Road" came through Tulsa through the support of Cyrus Avery, a Tulsan and member of the Oklahoma Highway Commission. The highway was scheduled to miss Tulsa, but Avery convinced leaders that construction would be less costly and more efficient by routing Route 66 across Tulsa's existing bridge over the Arkansas River. Route 66 was completed through Tulsa County in 1929. Delighted at a paved road, visitors attended dedication ceremonies during a rainstorm. Many drivers parked off the pavement and were mired for hours in the muddy shoulders.

Below: Bishop's Driv-Inn was conveniently located on Route 66, at Tenth Street and Boston Avenue.

After 1930, Oklahoma no longer was America's largest producer of oil as Texas and California produced large fields. By 1940, Oklahoma could claim to produce only about 10 percent of the nation's crude oil.

With reduced profits lingering from the Great Depression, many of Tulsa's pioneer oil men retired, leaving a huge gap of leadership in the county. However, one old-timer, Bill Skelly, remained a director of the Chamber of Commerce and helped lure defense industries to Tulsa, especially when it appeared that America would be pulled into World War II. In the months before Pearl Harbor in December, 1941, the War Department chose Tulsa as the site for a $15-million Douglas Aircraft Company plant. Tulsa voters approved, by an 11-to-1 margin, a $750,000 bond issue to close the deal with the War Department. When the plant opened, 10,000 Tulsans were hired to build Boeing B-24 bombers designed to carry the war to German Chancellor Adolf Hitler. The Douglas plant,

Top, left: The Philtower Building was built on the northeast corner of Fifth and Boston by oil money. It was constructed by oil man Waite Phillips, brother of Frank and L. E. Phillips, who founded the Phillips Petroleum Company. Waite was an outstanding independent oil man who gave his home, Philbrook, for future generations of Tulsans to enjoy.

Top, right: The Mayo Hotel opened for business in 1925 and became a favorite place of lodging for millionaire oil men who made their way to Tulsa.

Bottom, left: The Philcade Building was located on the southeast corner of Fifth Street and Boston Avenue.

Bottom, right: The interior hallways of the Philtower Building were elaborate with expensive lighting fixtures and ornate marble.

nearly one mile long, also built dive-bombers for use in the war in the Pacific and A-20 and A-26 Invaders for use in both Europe and the Pacific. Douglas workers also produced more than forty million pounds of military aircraft spare parts.

J. Paul Getty, who returned to Tulsa during World War II, used his Spartan Aircraft Company to get a share of the federal government's spending on producing airplanes. Spartan was open twenty-four hours a day, turning out an airplane a day. Spartan also produced many airplane parts such as wings and fuselages for a variety of airplane manufacturers during the war.

The Spartan School of Aeronautics played a major role in the war. Founded in 1928, the school helped General Jimmy Doolittle solve the U.S. Army's problem of America not having enough pilot training capacity at the

Top: The Akdar Theatre was built in 1934 at Fourth Street and Denver Avenue. It was a mosque for the Akdar Shrine but also was billed as "Oklahoma's Most Beautiful Playhouse." The theater opened with a Ziegfield Broadway musical production, Sally.

Middle: The Cosden Refinery provided hundreds of well-paying jobs for Tulsans.

Bottom: Tulsa's Little Theatre presented productions in a tent in 1928.

Opposite, top: One of the bright spots of the Great Depression was the completion of a lake in Tulsa's Mohawk Park. The project was one of many "make work" projects of the Works Progress Administration. Mohawk Park was once considered Oklahoma's greatest recreational center. It was a by-product of the construction of Mohawk Reservoir, Lake Yahola, to store water piped from Spavinaw Creek.

Opposite, bottom: Tulsa's skyline in 1936 showed the fruit of the oil boom, skyscrapers built by oil money.

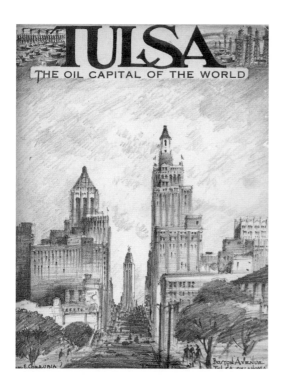

✧

Top, left: In 1937, the Tulsa Chamber of Commerce commissioned artist Paul E. Corrubia to draw scenes of Tulsa for a special book of illustrations. This was the cover drawing.

Bottom, left: Paul E. Corrubia's sketch of Will Rogers High School in 1937.

Right: Boston Avenue Methodist Church was built in 1929 and was quickly hailed as America's first skyscraper church.

beginning of the war. Thousands of U.S. pilots and mechanics were trained for America's flying forces.

When the Nazis attacked England, Spartan instructors trained hundreds of pilots to fly the Spitfires of the Royal Air Force (RAF). After Pearl Harbor, Spartan trained thousands of pilots for the RAF. The company was one of only nine private American companies approved by the Army Air Corps to train military pilots.

Tulsa County had barely held its own, population-wise, during the Great Depression. However, the county grew by nearly a third during World War II. A long decline in per capita income was reversed. By 1946 the per capita income was at $1,470, five times the average before the war. By the end of the war, retail sales and bank deposits skyrocketed.

Tulsa had survived some horrible days to become a great city again. Historian Angie Debo wrote, "Tulsa is the most American of American cities. All the forces that have gone into the making of the Republic have been intensified there. The successive stages through which the country as a whole has passed during three hundred years of history—Indian occupation, ranching, pioneering, industrial development, and finally disillusionment and the recasting of objectives—have been telescoped within the single lifetime of some of the older Tulsans. The result has been the quintessence of Americanism—its violence and strength, its buoyant optimism, its uncalculating generosity, its bumptious independence."

CHAPTER IV

A COSMOPOLITAN TOWN

At the end of the first generation of Tulsa's oil entrepreneurs, the county's leaders recognized they wanted a completely balanced city and county, where development of cultural, educational, and religious phases of the community were co-equal with industrial development, trade area expansion, and rising skylines.

Tulsa was chosen in 1946 as the headquarters for the United States Junior Chamber of Commerce (Jaycees). Landing such a prestigious organization caused Americans to sit up and take notice.

Tulsa had a cosmopolitan air—its foundation and population far different than Oklahoma's largest city, Oklahoma City. Part of the reason for Tulsa's unique persona was its attraction of high-paying professionals by the oil industry. By the 1950s the county was home to more engineers and scientists per capita than any other city in America.

Fortunately, for Tulsa's future, retiring oil men such as Waite Phillips shed their titles as captains of industry for a role as patrons of the arts. In 1938, Phillips gave his mansion, Villa Philbrook, to Tulsans for use as an art museum. He also donated the nine-story Beacon Building.

In 1944, Thomas Gilcrease, who gained his wealth as a 14-year-old holder of Creek property in the Glenn Pool strike, bought a huge collection of paintings by Charles Russell and Frederic Remington. Five years later, in 1949, the Gilcrease Museum opened, a showcase for the greatest privately-owned collection of Americana ever assembled. Gilcrease accumulated more than 200,000 items, including a Thomas Jefferson letter that expressed his thoughts on the eve of writing the Declaration of Independence.

In 1954, Gilcrease was in financial trouble and for awhile it seemed that his huge collection would have to be sold to pay creditors. But Alfred Aaronson, the son of a pioneer oil man, had other ideas. Aaronson convinced city leaders to present a bond issue to city voters-asking them to authorize the use of tax money to buy the Gilcrease Museum. Aaronson personally paid the $10,700 cost of the special election. Tulsans overwhelming approved the bond issue three-to-one.

In 1962, after Gilcrease's death, his family gave the city his home and surrounding property. Gilcrease expanded its collections and became one of America's great museums.

The Phillips and Gilcrease families were not the only families who continued to give back to Tulsa. In the last half of the twentieth century, major gifts to Tulsa County projects came from the Helmerich and Zarrow families and from other individuals and corporations that realized investment in Tulsa County would pay huge future dividends.

Music has always been an integral part of the fabric of the lives of the people who have inhabited Tulsa County. In 1934, Bob Wills and his band began broadcasting his unique blend of music called western swing. Fiddle tunes and ballads, performed by Wills and his Texas Playboys, put KVOO Radio on the map. Soon, Wills' western swing was the music of choice for millions of Americans.

For lovers of more "cultured" music, the Tulsa Philharmonic was created by H. Arthur Brown in 1949, the same year that Maude Lorton, the widow of Tulsa World publisher Eugene Lorton, formed the Tulsa Opera Club. In 1956, the Tulsa Civic Ballet, featuring Moscelyne Larkin and Roman Jasinski, gave its premier appearance in Temple Israel's Miller Auditorium. Larkin, a native Oklahoman, had met and married Jasinski while dancing with the Ballet Russe de Monte Carlo. The Tulsa Ballet Theatre became one of the country's most acclaimed dance companies.

Other forms of music are celebrated in Tulsa County. Tulsa's Greenwood District is home to the annual Jazz on Greenwood Festival that features local as well as nationally known jazz musicians. Greenwood has produced many talented blues artists. An annual bluegrass and chili festival

In 1990 the Philbrook Museum of Art was enlarged. A sculpture by Rodin was placed in a domed rotunda that linked the new building to the original home of Waite Phillips and his gardens.

attracts musicians and chili cooks to downtown Tulsa.

To create an excellent cultural atmosphere, Tulsa County schools excelled. The city and county's library system was greatly expanded when voters in 1962 approved the state's first tax levy explicitly for urban libraries. The tax money made possible a modern central library and five community branches.

Tulsa's black citizens rebounded from the ravages of the 1921 race riot to rebuild the Greenwood District into a thriving area. By the end of World War II, Greenwood boasted more than 200 block-owned and operated businesses. Few American cities could match Greenwood's experience of escaping the riot and the choking effect of the Great Depression.

The work of many paid off. In 1972, Fortune Magazine designated Tulsa as the second best of the nation's top fifty cities. Seattle, Washington, was first, but Tulsa was considered a better place to live and work than Dallas, New York City, and Chicago. Tulsa ranked well because of low crime, good healthcare, and the third highest rate of home ownership in the country. Tulsa's new name

became "All-American City" or "Magic City," replacing the earlier title of "oil capital of the world." Tulsa became an All-American city by broadening its economic base, transforming it from dependence upon a single industry—oil.

Along the way, Tulsa County leaders recognized the need for an adequate public water supply and an international airport. The Spavinaw water system was built in the 1920s and gave Tulsa freedom to greatly expand without fear of running out of water for its citizens and industries. The construction of

Tulsa International Airport gave Tulsa a fine facility to use as an attraction for new and expanding businesses. Government-sponsored road construction projects gave Tulsa County an enviable system of freeways and city streets.

Beginning in the 1960s, Tulsa's population began to shift to surrounding cities. The urban sprawl was unchecked, as mobile citizens used modern freeways to escape to newer neighborhoods. A barometer of the city's sprawl is the public school population.

Top, left: McGinty's Oklahoma Cowboy Band began appearing on KVOO Radio in 1925. It is thought to be America's first radio broadcast of a western string band.

Top, right: William Lewis, who appeared in 1948 in the first Tulsa Opera production, became a star at the Metropolitan Opera and other major opera houses.
COURTESY OF THE OKLAHOMA HERITAGE ASSOCIATION.

Below: Tulsa's Ernie Field's Orchestra gained national distinction in the world of jazz music from 1930 to 1950. Tulsa's Greenwood District was a hotbed of jazz musicians. The Clarence Love Lounge became a favorite spot for local jazz masters and stars such as Duke Ellington, Louis Armstrong, and Woody Herman. Music scholars call Greenwood Jazz the foundation of the Kansas City School of Jazz. Many musicians who played on Greenwood Avenue became world famous.

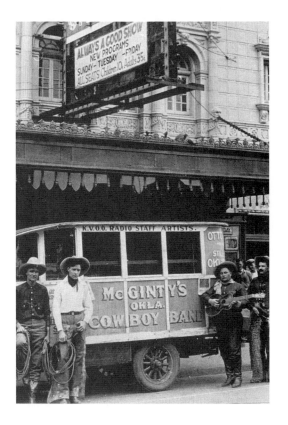

By 1990, Tulsa schools had lost more than half its 1960 enrollment while suburban schools became huge. The Jenks school district had more students than the city of Jenks had citizens. The Union district in Broken Arrow became one of the largest school

✧

Top: Tulsa County citizens were proud of
the area's natural beauty, but added to the
beauty with the construction of a rose
garden at Tulsa's Woodward Park.

Middle: The wading pool at Central Park
in Tulsa.

Bottom: The Bama Pie Company began
business in 1937 in Tulsa under the tutelage
of Paul Marshall who inherited the idea
from his mother who had sold homemade
pies in Dallas a decade earlier. This is a
photograph of Bama employees outside the
company plant at Eleventh Street and
Delaware Avenue in 1943.

Below: Evangelist Oral Roberts made Tulsa
his headquarters as he became America's
most famous television preacher. Roberts
established Oral Roberts University in 1964.
COURTESY OF ORAL ROBERTS UNIVERSITY.

 Top: Instructors at the Spartan School of Aeronautics trained thousands of pilots during World War II. Tulsa's Harvey Young Airport served as a training center for the overflow. In this photograph, rookie pilots wait to take to the air.

Middle: A skyline view of Tulsa in 1954 with the DX Refinery in the foreground.

Bottom, left: Pennington's Drive-In at Forty-second Place and South Peoria Avenue in 1955.

Below: Tulsa always has been a baseball town. A. Ray Smith owned the Tulsa Oilers minor league team in the 1960s and 1970s. When he moved the Class AAA Oilers to New Orleans before the 1977 season, Tulsa was faced with no professional baseball. Building contractor Bill Rollings obtained the Texas Rangers AA team from Lafayette, Louisiana, and Tulsa re-entered the Texas League. In a fan contest, "Drillers" was selected as a nickname.

COURTESY OF THE TULSA DRILLERS.

districts in the state. In the 1990s and in the early years of the new century, Jenks and Union produced outstanding football teams, often battling for the right to be called state champion.

Following patterns in most American urban centers, the growth of suburban communities in Tulsa County left its ugly imprint on Tulsa's most vibrant commercial district. Empty shopping centers in the inner city and dilapidated sections of buildings in north Tulsa signaled the need for a better plan. Although Tulsa County leaders had worked feverishly for decades to prevent what happened, they now begged for more aggressive and modern plans of action.

✧

Left: Completion of Keystone Reservoir west of Tulsa was near when this photograph was taken in 1964.

Below: Tulsa's sprawling downtown area in 1967.

CHAPTER V

THE MAGIC EMPIRE

The word "magic" has long been associated with Tulsa County. President Theodore Roosevelt called Tulsa "a magic city" in 1910. World War I army hero General John J. Pershing, called Tulsa the "wonder city of the world." Fancy names were easy to come by when oil gushed from the ground in the county in such quantities that technology strained to keep up with production.

Tulsa's oil heritage was displayed in the 1949 movie, *Tulsa*, starring Susan Hayward and Robert Preston. However, as oil and gas played a lesser role in the economy in the last part of the twentieth century, Tulsa County diversified its commercial base. Tulsa was the state's second largest metropolitan area and began to exert its political muscle.

In 1966, Republican Dewey Bartlett became the first governor of Oklahoma from Tulsa. In 1970 it was Tulsan against Tulsan. Bartlett ran for re-election, but was defeated by Democrat David Hall, the former county attorney in Tulsa County. Later, in 1994, Tulsa lawyer Frank Keating was elected to the first of two terms as a popular governor of Oklahoma.

In the 1970s the Port of Catoosa and the Arkansas River Navigation Project were completed, although dreams for such a gargantuan undertaking had been born in major floods three decades before. Navigation of the Arkansas River was the dream of one man, Robert S. Kerr. As governor of Oklahoma in 1943, Kerr had surveyed the devastation of an Arkansas River flood that took nearly three dozen lives and covered 2,300 square miles of mostly farm and pastureland.

Kerr made the Arkansas River his issue. After he was elected to the United States Senate in 1948, he joined forces with Arkansas Senator John McClellan. Both envisioned development of the Arkansas River. Kerr and Tulsa Congressman Page Belcher created a bloc of supporters in Congress that ultimately approved more than $1 billion of federal expenditures to build the Tulsa Port of Catoosa and the McClellan-Kerr Arkansas River Navigation System. The project was the third largest public works project in American history—exceeded only by the Panama Canal and the Apollo Space Program.

History has not yet recorded the total positive impact of the Arkansas River Navigation System, even though there is no doubt that many jobs were created and Tulsa County's economy was greatly boosted. New towns were built to serve the needs of campers and tourists and support the efforts of workers who shipped millions of tons of freight from the Port of Catoosa to the waiting commercial world.

When the Port of Catoosa began operation in 1972, Tulsa became the state's leader in manufacturing, with a well-trained workforce that exceeded the manufacturing jobs claimed by a much larger Oklahoma City.

On January 4, 1979, George Nigh, who had been elected to succeed David Boren as governor, was sworn in at the Downtown Tulsa Mall to complete the five days remaining in Boren's term after he was elected to the United States Senate. It is the only time a governor of Oklahoma has been sworn into office in Tulsa.

In the final decade of the century, former Tulsa Mayor James Inhofe served as one of Oklahoma's two United States senators.

Tulsa leaders majestically mixed old Art Deco-Style structures with new construction that changed the city's skyline. When completed in 1973, the forty-two-story First National BanCorporation Tower, between Boston Avenue and Main Street in downtown Tulsa, was the state's tallest building.

Sid Patterson's Up With Trees organization has planted more than twelve thousand trees on Tulsa County's roads and highways since the program began when Patterson was Tulsa's street commissioner.

✧

Dewey Bartlett was the first Tulsa County resident to be elected governor of Oklahoma. Bartlett later served in the United States Senate. In this photograph, Bartlett's widow, Ann, unveils a portrait of her husband following his death in 1979.

Southern Hills Country Club had one of America's finest and most recognized golf courses, hosting major events such as the U.S. Open, the PGA, and National Amateur golf championships.

In the early 1980s, the Union Railroad Depot was restored to its original grandeur of a half-century before. When the facility opened at the intersection of Third Street and Boulder Avenue in 1931, it was the first Union depot in the state.

The boom and bust of the oil patch increased Tulsa County's effort to diversify its economic base in the 1980s. In the decade before, the increased price of oil pumped unheard-of excitement into the board rooms of Tulsa's oil and gas companies. Because of the fear that foreign suppliers would cut off America's great demand for petroleum, Oklahoma oil men headed for the time-worn fields, drilling new wells and re-working old ones.

Oil men hardly slept—banks loaned money as quickly as they could. As the price of crude oil jumped, new fortunes were being made, reminiscent of early-day Tulsa County when aggressive wildcatters became wealthy and began giving back to their community. Everyone wanted to be in the oil business again—many had a brand new Mercedes in their garage as a symbol of the new-found wealth of oil.

However, in 1984, dreams of $80-a-barrel oil burst. In a matter of weeks, the world oil price slid to $13 per barrel. The fall of Oklahoma City's Penn Square Bank, a bank that history shows could hardly say no to any oil deal during the boom, reverberated through Tulsa County and the rest of the nation. During an 18-month period, Tulsa County lost more than 40,000 jobs.

Tulsa County leaders were resilient and used the oil bust as a platform from which to preach economic diversification. Tulsa city leaders set

a goal of creating thirty-six thousand new jobs within a decade. By the end of the 1980s the plan was working—ten thousand jobs had been created by high tech and manufacturing companies that had relocated to Tulsa County. Officials cited the addition of another thirty thousand jobs created through the expansion of existing businesses and development of home-grown small businesses.

The transformation from an oil-based economy to a wide range of industries was profound. One company that had been in the oil field supply business began making fitness machines. Because of Tulsa County's low cost of living and highly qualified labor force, city and county leaders were able to convince national and international companies to locate plants and divisions in the county.

Older Tulsa County companies had to reinvent themselves. An example is the Williams Brothers Companies that had its roots in concrete construction in 1908, and

later became a national leader in pipeline construction. Under the guidance of a new generation of Williams, the company entered the world of telecommunications and became a world leader in that arena.

Much of Tulsa County's success in attracting business was founded upon a strong educational system. At the beginning of the twenty-first century, nearly one-fourth of Tulsa's residents held at least a bachelor's degree. The city was filled with fine institutions. Henry Kendall College, now the University of Tulsa, is a nationally recognized private university. In the mid-1960s, evangelist Oral Roberts established Oral Roberts University in south Tulsa. Tulsa Junior College, now Tulsa Community College, opened in 1970. A branch of the University of Oklahoma was housed in Tulsa, as was the Oklahoma State University College of Osteopathic Medicine.

However, for most of the twentieth century, Tulsa was the largest metropolitan area in the nation without a state-supported institution of comprehensive higher education. Because of the excellence of the private universities and Tulsa Community College, with its four campuses and highly-rated curriculum, the idea for a state-supported institution of higher

learning in Tulsa did not traditionally fare well with the Oklahoma legislature.

A start was the University Center in Tulsa—a combined effort of the University of Oklahoma, Oklahoma State University, Langston University, and Northeastern Oklahoma State University to offer classes on a new campus in the Greenwood District just north of downtown Tulsa. The University Center merged for a short time with Rogers State College at Claremore, under the name of Rogers University.

After much discussion, Tulsa's need for a public higher education campus was finally realized with the January 1, 1999, opening of Oklahoma State University-Tulsa, an urban campus of the major state university based in Stillwater. It is estimated that OSU-Tulsa will have twenty thousand students by the year 2020.

Tulsa County has a system of strong public and private elementary, middle, and high schools. In 2005, the Tulsa school district was the largest public school district in Oklahoma. Public schools in the fifteen other districts in

✧

Above: Downtown Tulsa in 1972.

Right: Tulsa, with the Arkansas River in the foreground.

Left: Deano's Wandering Polka Band took part in the 1978 Great Raft Race on the Arkansas River. The annual event drew huge crowds and innovative rafts. Some floated—some did not.

COURTESY OF THE OKLAHOMA PUBLISHING COMPANY.

Below: At age fourteen, Paul Aurandt was taken by his English teacher to KVOO Radio when it was located at the top of the Philtower Building. Isabel Ronan said, "This young man has the talent and ability to be on your radio station." She was right, Paul changed his last name to Harvey and spent many decades on ABC Radio as one of America's favorite news commentators. Paul Harvey's father was a Tulsa police officer who was killed in the line of duty when Paul was three years old.

COURTESY OF THE OKLAHOMA PUBLISHING COMPANY.

surrounding towns in the county have registered huge gains over the past two decades as new neighborhoods have been built and population increased. The Tulsa public school district is the county's second-largest employer.

Higher education in Tulsa County is complemented by the Tulsa Technology Center (TTC). On four campuses and three satellite-training centers, instructors at TTC teach vocational skills to more than 30,000 county high school students and work with industrial development leaders to custom-design training programs for new or expanding private industry

CHAPTER VI

A VISION FOR A NEW CENTURY

At the beginning of the twenty-first century, oil was still an important part of the economic landscape of Tulsa County, although decades of ups and downs in the petroleum industry had lessened its impact. In fact, the periods of boom and bust had caused county leaders to emphasize diversification.

In the 1990s, Tulsa was highly successful in attracting industries from telecommunications to aerospace. Such diversification ended decades of boom and bust cycles and birthed unprecedented opportunity for the creation of new and higher-paying jobs for Tulsa County citizens.

By 2005, companies based in Tulsa County generated more than sixty percent of the entire state's exports. Workforce development programs utilized by Tulsa County companies were emulated across the country as industrial development leaders recognized Tulsa's success.

Tulsa County, however, offered more than just new jobs for potential new citizens. A symphony orchestra, an internationally acclaimed opera company, a world-famous ballet company, two world-class museums, and theater opportunities not available in most American cities, added to the quality of life that Tulsa Countians could experience.

The first test of the county's new diversified economy came in the mid-1990s when plummeting oil prices again dominated the headlines. There was no monumental loss of jobs as in previous busts—the new Tulsa County economy was able to absorb job cuts by oil and gas firms into the new workforce.

In the final years of the twentieth century, many national companies established their presence in Tulsa County, including Avis, Ford Glass, Blue Bell Creameries, Metropolitan Life Insurance Company, Citgo Petroleum, Dollar Thrifty Automotive, State Farm Insurance Companies, TV Guide, and Whirlpool Corporation. When Whirlpool announced its major home appliance manufacturing plant would be located in the county, other companies took note of the partnership between local governments and educational facilities to provide a well-trained labor pool.

Many hi-tech companies have joined the Tulsa County economy. The Cherokee Industrial Park, located seven miles north of downtown Tulsa, is home to more than 4,000 employees of MCI WorldCom, a unique international company that provides local, long distance, and Internet services. The company is the second largest telephone long distance provider in the United States.

Tulsa County has excelled in providing quality health care for its citizens. Tulsa Hospital opened in 1906 and quickly became recognized in the region as a quality provider of medical services. In 1916, Hillcrest Hospital began admitting patients. A decade later, St. John Hospital was founded by the Sisters of the Sorrowful Mother, and the Junior League of Tulsa established Children's Medical Center to care for the city's poor children.

In 1940, Tulsa entered a contest with Oklahoma City to see which city would be the first to raise $5,000 to establish a new prepaid hospitalization plan. The winning city would be the headquarters of the new group. Tulsa won. The headquarters of Group Hospital Service, now Blue Cross Blue Shield of Oklahoma, the state's largest health insurance carrier, was located, and remains, in Tulsa.

In 1960, oil man W. K. Warren, and his wife, Natalie, helped create the Saint Francis Health System. In the four decades since the facility opened, Saint Francis has grown to include a psychiatric hospital, the Warren Clinic, and Broken Arrow Medical Center.

Contributing to the quality of medical care for Tulsa County citizens are two medical schools, the Oklahoma State University College of Osteopathic Medicine and the University of Oklahoma (OU) College of Medicine-Tulsa. The OU facility was opened in 1999 in the former BP-Amoco Tulsa Technology Center.

❖

One of Tulsa County's major employers is American Airlines that maintains its fleet of aircraft at facilities adjacent to Tulsa International Airport. The annual American Airlines payroll in Tulsa County is approaching a half-billion dollars.

COURTESY OF THE OKLAHOMA PUBLISHING COMPANY.

At the end of the twentieth century, nearly one in ten Tulsa County employees worked in the medical field or in related jobs. Saint Francis, St. John, and Hillcrest hospitals were among the top twenty employers in Tulsa. CommunityCare Managed Care Plans of Oklahoma, a joint effort of St. John and Saint Francis hospitals and two Oklahoma City hospitals, was Oklahoma's first provider-owned health maintenance organization.

In 2003, Tulsa County voters approved "Vision 2025," a forward-looking proposal for capital improvements and economic development for the next decade. A 6/10 of a penny increase in the county sales tax will fund 33 projects at a total cost of $530 million. Tulsa County leaders believe Vision 2025 will create thousands of new jobs, enhance educational opportunities for citizens, stimulate millions of dollars in private investment, spur growth of small businesses, and unlock the potential of the region.

Vision 2025 was not the first time that the city of Tulsa and Tulsa County had formed a partnership to provide services for residents. In previous decades, the city and county partnered to build a world-class library system, health department, and jail.

Vision 2025 projects include major road and highway construction, renovation of downtown Tulsa neighborhoods and the Sand Springs Keystone industrial corridor,

significant improvements to Mohawk Park, flood prevention, a new community center for Broken Arrow, reconstruction of the Collinsville city hall, construction of an Oklahoma Jazz Hall of Fame, building parks and trails, a community center and medical complex in Owasso, community centers in Sperry and Skiatook, relocation of the Tulsa Air and Space Museum, capital support for the Oklahoma Aquarium at Jenks, and a state-of-the-art health care facility in north Tulsa.

Education will be the beneficiary of millions of dollars of funds from Vision 2025 sales tax

✧

Above: Swans feeding at the edge of the Arkansas River.

Below: Siberian tigers bathing at their home in the Tulsa Zoo that opened in 1928 with 35 animals. In 2005 the zoo managed more than 4,000 animals and 500 different species.

revenues. Space will be built for 4,000 more students at Northeastern Oklahoma State University Broken Arrow. Langston University-Tulsa will have new facilities to meet the expected doubling of its enrollment. A new medical biotechnology-learning center will be built on the southeast campus of Tulsa Community College. Oklahoma State University-Tulsa will receive $30 million for the construction of an advanced technology research center that will attract scholars and researchers from around the world. The

University of Oklahoma-Tulsa will receive an equal amount for the construction of a research, medical, and clinical care facility to extend service to medically needy citizens of the county.

The largest projects included in the Vision 2025 package are for Expo Square and the Tulsa Regional Convention/Events Center. Expo Square, the state's busiest events complex, will receive $40 million to add parking facilities, a livestock barn, a new exchange center building, grandstand enclosure, and related improvements. Expo

✧

Above: QuikTrip Corporation of Tulsa has become a leading gasoline retailer in America.

Below: The Donald W. Reynolds Center is home for University of Tulsa sporting events, concerts, and other campus and community events.

Square holds more than 400 events each year, attended by 3.5 million people. Three fourths of the citizens of Tulsa County attend at least one event annually at Expo Square.

The Tulsa Regional Convention/Events Center will get a much needed modernization of new construction of an 18,000-seat events center that can be used for concerts and sports events. Leaders estimate that the updated convention center will make Tulsa a more attractive venue for conventions and trade shows and will generate near $6 million annually in state and local tax revenues.

Advances in making Tulsa County a better place to live and work have brought national recognition. In 2004, Partners for Livable Communities selected Tulsa as one of America's "Most Livable Communities." Tulsa was cited for its unsurpassed beauty, a well-educated workforce, cultural diversity, and a pro-business environment. Tulsa has the second shortest commute time of major American cities and ranked fifteenth in the nation for the highest rate of high school graduation.

A significant factor in Tulsa being named one of the nation's most livable cities was the comparison between cost of living and median income. Tulsa County's cost of living was eight percent below the national average while the county's per capita income was $27,654, 11 percent above the national average.

The history of Tulsa County is rich in heritage—and its future is bold and bright.

Tulsa World *has sponsored the*
Tulsa Run *since its inception. The annual*
event has become one of the premiere
fifteen-hundred-kilometer races in the
United States.
<small>COURTESY OF THE *TULSA WORLD.*</small>

Chapter VII

Other Places We Call Home

BROKEN ARROW

When Broken Arrow was primarily a farming community, chicken farmers culled their flocks and brought their roosters to town to sell. After poultry trading became a thing of the past, the rooster became a symbol of Broken Arrow's past and continues to be the theme of an annual spring celebration appropriately called "Rooster Days."

Broken Arrow was founded on October 16, 1902, named for an original Creek Indian town, Broken Arrow, Alabama. The Broken Arrow Creeks were a branch of the Muskogees of the Creek Nation and made the long journey to Indian Territory in 1831. When they established their new settlement in what would become Oklahoma, they named it Broken Arrow, the westernmost Creek settlement that could be found in journals of pioneer surveyors of the West.

In 1832, Washington Irving visited Broken Arrow. In his book, *A Tour on the Prairies*, Irving described Broken Arrow, "For some miles the country was sprinkled with Creek villages and farm houses, the inhabitants of which appeared to have adopted, with considerable facility, the rudiments of civilization and to have thriven in consequence. Their farms are well stocked and their house had a look of comfort and abundance."

After the Civil War, in which the Creeks allied with the Confederacy, whites began moving onto the land around Broken Arrow. Texas cattlemen, driving their herds to railheads in Kansas, passed through Broken Arrow. It was not unusual for the town to have hundreds of guest-campers for the night. William P. Moore established a trading post in 1874, signaling an influx of non-Indians.

By 1900 the Creek settlement at Weir Springs, southeast of present day Broken Arrow, no longer existed. Trees that had surrounded the old Creek town square were visible, even though buildings had faded into the pastureland. Several small towns—Fry, Evans, and Oneta—had sprung up in the area to serve the farmers who still lived there.

In 1901, W. T. Brooks, N. L. Sanders, W. N. "Newt" Williams, and M. C. "Mac" Williams, built a general store and cotton gin in the middle of a cotton patch where they envisioned the railroad would soon be laid. In 1902, W. S. Fears, secretary of the Arkansas Valley Townsite Company, bought land at the heart of present Broken Arrow from the Missouri-Kansas-Texas Railroad. Because the original 120-acre town site was in the old Creek community, Fears named the new town, Broken Arrow. Early settlers lived in tents until they could buy building materials for permanent dwellings.

Broken Arrow grew overnight. Once the plat was approved, H. W. Raupe bought the first lot the following day. Two new stores opened for business that day. The first business was the O.K. Restaurant, opened in a tent on South Main Street a few days before the official plat was recorded. The Brady brothers opened the restaurant and served hamburgers cooked on a wood stove to potential lot buyers. Early families that played important roles in Broken Arrow's development were the McIntoshes, Perrymans, and Childers. The first house built on the Broken Arrow townsite was erected by the Hammond Lumber Company to be used as an office.

The Katy Railroad reached Broken Arrow on April 16, 1903, built primarily to haul coal that was being mined from shallow pits. The train depot was constructed the following month and received new residents moving to the town.

Agriculture was the mainstay of the economy and new Broken Arrow citizens opted to move into the countryside to till the land. A 1903 editorial in the *Broken Arrow Ledger* called the town a "beautiful, productive, healthful locality." The newspaper said, "Standing on a picturesque mound half a mile to the northeast of the village, one may gaze over one of the most beautiful agricultural portions of the United States." What viewers saw was a broad, level valley dotted with wheat fields.

✧

Broken Arrow's Main Street, c. 1906.

COURTESY OF THE TULSA COUNTY HISTORICAL SOCIETY.

6302 PUBLIC SCHOOL, BROKEN ARROW, I. T

Broken Arrow was incorporated on May 4, 1903. J. B. Parkinson was the first mayor and Tom Higgins was the first marshal. Schools and churches were built to make a quality life available for old and new residents alike. As talk of statehood for Indian Territory and Oklahoma Territory increased, Broken Arrow attempted to become the county seat in one of the proposed counties of the state of Sequoyah. Broken Arrow won an election over Coweta to become the county seat of Coweta County of the proposed Sequoyah.

Congress squashed any idea of two states and officially approved the idea to admit Oklahoma as the forty-sixth state. When county lines were drawn for the new state, Tulsa became Broken Arrow's foe and ultimately was selected as the county seat of Tulsa County. Broken Arrow residents had offered to donate a two-story brick building for a county courthouse, and were bitterly disappointed when the constitutional convention named Tulsa as the county seat.

By the 1920s, Broken Arrow was a bustling community that had four large grain elevators, two cotton gins, flour and corn mills, three banks, a soda pop factory, three hotels, dozens of other businesses, three lawyers, and four doctors.

Eventually, Broken Arrow's economy turned from agriculture to a more broad-based, diverse economy. The city's first major industry was Braden Winch Company that moved its plant from Tulsa to Broken Arrow in 1945. Many other manufacturing firms followed, providing high paying jobs for Broken Arrow residents. Broken Arrow became Oklahoma's fifth largest city by 1990, quadrupling its population of just twenty years before.

Blue Bell Creameries built an ice cream plant in Broken Arrow in 1990, one of three such facilities in the nation. By 2000, Broken Arrow was the state's third largest manufacturing city, home to more than two hundred facilities that made everything from machine tools to furniture. FlightSafety International, Inc., provided hundreds of high-tech jobs and made Broken Arrow the flight simulator capital of the world.

Broken Arrow remained the state's fifth largest city in the 2000 census with a population of 74,859.

SAND SPRINGS

Sand Springs was the creation of one man—Charles Page. At about the time Oklahoma was preparing for statehood, Page, an oil man and entrepreneur, bought 160 acres west of Tulsa in an area known for its clear water from "sandy springs" along the north bank of the Arkansas River. Page's idea was to build a planned industrial community to provide a source of perpetual funding for an orphanage and widows colony he founded. In 1909 he had been appointed guardian of twenty-five orphans who were left homeless by the bankruptcy of the Cross and Anchor Orphanage in Tulsa. He transported the children by wagon from Tulsa to land near the sandy springs and housed them in tents until he could have small cottages built.

When Page arrived, what would become the booming town of Sand Springs was nothing but a sandy wilderness occupied by a few Native American families. In 1908, Page began purchasing land from Creek Indians, some tracts for just $35 an acre. He offered free land to industries that would move into the area to provide jobs.

The first dormitory of the Sand Springs Home was built in 1910. Page believed in teaching the children trades. In a Manual Arts Training Building built of sandstone in 1916, boys were taught to build and repair wagons, farm implements, and furniture. Page was highly successful in raising money to add buildings for the growing number of children who came to live at what he called "The Home." Thousands of children were served by the Sand Springs Home until 1991.

Page's plan for Sand Springs was successful. As new businesses came, houses were built for workers. A post office was established on September 5, 1911. The town was incorporated one year later.

Page built a transportation system, provided a good water supply, and electric power to attract new industries. Years ahead of others in the field of industrial development, Page offered a $20,000 resettlement bonus to companies relocating in Sand Springs. He also enticed businesses with the promise of low utilities and a pro-business city atmosphere that contributed to Sand Springs becoming the "Industrial Center of the Southwest."

From its beginning, Sand Springs enjoyed a diverse economy. The Imperial Manufacturing Company manufactured some of the first electric washing machines in America. VIGO Dog Food and Empire Chandelier joined other companies that produced a variety of consumer products. By

1914, more than 1,200 people lived in Sand Springs and worked for the Pheonix and Pierce oil refineries and dozens of other plants that sprang up like weeds on the sandy prairie. Kerr Glass revolutionized fruit and vegetable canning with its patented "self-sealing" jar.

The Sand Springs Home built a $1-million cotton mill in 1923. Eventually, the facility became Commander Mills, the largest factory of its kind west of the Mississippi River until production was scaled down in the 1960s.

Page, who died unexpectedly in 1926, realized his dream of Sand Springs having a steel mill when Osage Iron and Steel moved to

❖

Above: Oklahoma Governor J. Howard Edmondson, at podium, presides over the groundbreaking for the Broken Arrow Expressway on July 29, 1960.

Below: Fourteen-year-old Broken Arrow singer Kristin Chenoweth does some last minute primping at the Oklahoma Diamond Jubilee Kids Talent Search in 1982. After college, Chenoweth became a major Broadway and television star.
COURTESY OF THE OKLAHOMA PUBLISHING COMPANY.

Right: The Sand Springs Home for orphans, built and maintained by philanthropist Charles Page.

Below: Charles Page, center, poses with several of the girls who were residents of the Sand Springs Home in 1925. The children called Page, "Daddy Page," and he often referred to the children as "his kids."

the community in 1913. When the company closed, the Sand Springs Home continued its operation until the facility could be leased to Tulsa Rolling Mills, and later Sheffield Steel Company, a subsidiary of ARMCO. After World War II, ARMCO made improvements to the plant that became a world leader in casting efficiency.

Sand Springs has operated under a council manager form of city government since 1969. The city's population in 2000 was 17,451.

Residents of Sand Springs, nestled in the steep and wooded hills bordering the Arkansas River, liked to be called "Sandites," and are proud of their heritage. From the great plans of self-made millionaire, Charles Page, the city used its diverse industrial base to endure the Great Depression, two world wars, and continues in the twenty-first century as a thriving part of Tulsa County.

SKIATOOK

William C. Rogers opened a small store on the present site of Skiatook in 1880. Rogers, a Cherokee, was the grandson of Captain John Rogers, a friend of President Andrew Jackson,

Above: The Sand Springs Railway was the lifeblood of the community until it closed in 1955. Streetcars provided a critical connection between Sand Springs and Tulsa's business district, carrying freight, tourists, and workers. It was a rarity, a rail line owned and operated by a philanthropic organization, the Sand Springs Home.

Below: Civil defense workers assess water damage to a Sand Springs business after a devastating flood on the Arkansas River in 1943.

THE WOODHOUSE VISIT

S. W. Woodhouse, a young Philadelphia physician and avid ornithologist, accompanied government surveyors on expeditions in 1849 and 1850 to survey the Creek-Cherokee boundary in Indian Territory. Woodhouse was a keen observer of frontier life and society, writing in his journals incredibly detailed descriptions of the flora and fauna as well as the people and places he visited in Indian Territory. In 1849 he spent several days in what would become Tulsa County. Here are excerpts from his journals:

(September 12) Captain and I took a ride to hunt a place for our next camp…rode about 3 miles and a half, found a rode leading most of the way suitable for a wagon. Moses traded Proud Bill, a Creek Indian, for a Comanche pony. In the afternoon, I overhauled my collection of plants and dined at 4 o'clock off roast wild turkey which we bought from an Indian for 3 for 50 cents…

(September 13) I shouldered my gun and took the dogs and walked to the Arkansas River. This I found very low and more than half of the river dry. The bottom consists of white sand much resembling the sea shore only it was much more solid which I suppose was caused by its being intermixed with clay. On my return my attention was attracted by the old dog, he having found something in an old hollow tree lying on the ground. I commenced poking in it with a stick and I found the animal commenced growling…I found it was an opossum. Then I renewed my punching for some time, holding the dog with my other hand, he finding his situation very uncomfortable, rushed out when he dogs seized him. I walked several miles but found nothing worth shooting and returned to camp at noon.

There was an Osage stopped here this afternoon…he was not troubled much with cloathing having nothing on but a breech clout…his hair was cut close to his scull excepting a scalp lock and was painted with Vermilion, his ears were slit and filled with beads. From signs he made me, he gave to understand that there were a great many of them crossing the Red fork (Cimarron) and that they were on their way hunting buffalo. In the evening, I took a bath.

(September 14) We then rode over a prairie…when we entered the timber and followed over some rocky hills of limestone. On the trail we met some Creeks and endeavored by means of signs…I purchased a buckskin for 25 cents. One of them led us to the spot where they were assembled. The women were by themselves eating, the men having finished. One portion of the young men were playing cards and the little boys were playing ball and one of the men teaching them…

They had on one side a scaffold, under which there had been a large fire on which there was placed a beef cut in pieces and roasted. We seated ourselves on a log and then one of the squas brought the leg bone with a quantity of meat on it and placed it on some leaves on the ground before us and a plate with some good corn bread. This beef was very fine and fat…We then took a smoke with them and looked at the little fellows playing ball…It was getting late and we bid them farewell. They tried to persuade us to stay as they were going to have a dance, but we did not like to encounter the river in the night.

The location of this painting by Wayne Cooper, on display at the Oklahoma State Capitol, is looking across the Arkansas River from present-day Sand Springs. In 1849, surgeon and naturalist S. W. Woodhouse accompanied government surveyors as they plotted the Creek-Cherokee boundary in Indian Territory. Woodhouse was an expert in birds and wildlife and spotted a scissortail flycatcher that would become Oklahoma's official state bird nearly a century later. The region in the painting is called "Lost City" because the huge limestone boulders resemble a village from the distance.

who brought the first organized band of Cherokees west of the Mississippi in 1814. Young Rogers stood more than six feet and was later elected principal chief of the Cherokee Nation.

When Rogers first opened his store, there was no post office in the community, forcing him to travel to the nearest railroad station for supplies and to receive and dispatch mail. Unfortunately, the nearest station was Coffeyville, Kansas. With the help of federal government officials, Rogers was able to obtain an official post office, named Ski-a-took, that opened on March 12, 1880.

Historians disagree as to how Skiatook received its name. Colonel Clarence B. Douglas, who published a three-volume history of Tulsa in 1921, cites personal interviews with Rogers and says Ski-a-took is a compound word taken from the Cherokee language, which is "generally accepted as meaning Big-Injun-Me." Douglas reported that Rogers said the word also may refer to something large, like a large man, a vast tract of land, or the camp of some other tribe of Indians.

On the other hand, historian George Shirk, in his 1965 book, *Oklahoma Place*

Names, says Skiatook was named for Skiatooka, a prominent Osage, whose community around his homestead was known as Skiatooka's Settlement.

On April 11, 1092, the official name of the post office was changed to the present spelling of Skiatook. Rogers' store did booming business and Skiatook became a well established landmark and convenient trading point for travelers headed northeast from Tulsa.

The town of Skiatook had its beginning on December 18, 1904, as families settled the area around Rogers' store. The first deed granted in the town went to the Skiatook Bank, and before nightfall on December 18, seven loads of lumber were sent to construct a building to house the bank. People lived in tents and shacks. Tents also housed new businesses such as O'Brill Drug Store, Dickason-Goodman Lumber Company, and the Feigly and Son general merchandise and hardware store. Colonel Douglas wrote of Skiatook's early days, "Through a severe winter all kept in a good humour, and when nothing else could be found for amusement, the good old-fashioned square dance, frontier style, came in for its place. Everybody worked

✧

Kerr Glass Company of Sand Springs operated a fleet of promotional cars in 1938 to teach canning and promote the use of Kerr jars.

from the earliest break of day until the last ray of light had faded into darkness."

Pioneers of Skiatook put up buildings in record time, awaiting construction of a railroad to the village. Businesses were well established by the time the first train arrived in May, 1905. After the arrival of rail service, more people moved into the Skiatook area, prompting a boom in residential building.

Skiatook was incorporated in the summer of 1905. A. E. Townsend was the first mayor. Joseph Mercer was the first chief of police. A local gas company and a public telephone system provided service to residences beginning in 1906. Local roads were still primitive—wagons and early motor vehicles had to ford streams without bridges. At statehood, money for roads became available.

Permanent sidewalks appeared in 1909. In 1911 a fire destroyed a half city block of buildings. However, Skiatook citizens quickly rebuilt the area. The following year, water, sewer, and electric systems were funded by voters and added much to the quality of life in the town.

Rapid development increased traffic to the point where dirt streets became impassable during spring rains. By the fall of 1919, Skiatook boasted fifteen blocks of continuous concrete-paved streets.

In 1951, Skiatook purchased the electrical distribution system in the town from Public Service Company of Oklahoma. The town buys its electricity from the Grand River Dam Authority. The purchasing of the electric system was a wise financial decision for Skiatook, enabling city leaders to expand services without a sales tax increase.

Since its inception, Skiatook has offered small-town living with immediate access to a large city. In fact, voters have turned down attempts to make the town an official city. Skiatook is four miles east of Skiatook Lake and only one half hour from downtown Tulsa.

OWASSO

Early residents of Owasso were convinced their town was named for an Indian word, but confusion exists as to which tribe. Early historians wrote that Owasso, an Osage word meaning "the end," derived its name when the community was literally at the end of the Atchison, Topeka, and Santa Fe Railroad in

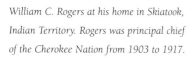

William C. Rogers at his home in Skiatook, Indian Territory. Rogers was principal chief of the Cherokee Nation from 1903 to 1917.

Indian Territory. Others said Owasso is a derivation of a Cherokee word.

In any event, the first building in the town was the Santa Fe Depot, constructed in 1897. Preston Ballard was the first permanent resident of Owasso. He moved his house from Elm post office, a nearby crossroads store.

The town was surveyed and platted in 1897 when reports circulated that Owasso would become a Santa Fe division point. Buildings sprang up overnight, fueled by Santa Fe's construction of a small lake as a water supply for its steam engines. Some of the first businessmen were grocers B. F. Finch and J. B. Taylor; N. R. Mounger, manager of the W. O. Whitney Lumber Company; hotel keeper W. L. Smith; and druggist J. C. Chany.

In 1898, the Ballard and Overturf General Store opened to a booming business. Later the Smith Brothers store served customers within a ten-mile radius of Owasso. In a meeting room over the Smith Brothers store, the Woodmen of the World became the town's first fraternal organization.

Eight miles northeast of Tulsa, the Owasso post office was established January 24, 1900. Several pioneer families banded together to raise money at box suppers to provide funds for a school building and church. Three men sawed timbers from the Bird Creek bottom for the school's foundation. N. D. Smith, a twenty-two-year-old graduate of the Cherokee Male Seminary, volunteered to start the first Owasso School. Parents paid $1 a month for classes that began in the fall of 1900.

In 1904, the Santa Fe extended its line to Tulsa, and Owasso finally became a division point on the railway line. Because all trains stopped at Owasso, two hotels were built—the Eureka and the Palace. C. O. Kinney, the owner of the Palace Hotel, was a key promoter of Owasso, although his hotel burned in 1907.

Two grain elevators were built in 1905 to store large crops grown within a few miles of the town. Within a short time, the elevators of the Caney Grain Company and Dickson Brothers were filled to capacity and thousands of bushels of grain were piled on vacant lots around the town.

The oil boom changed the landscape on some of the Owasso area farms. At first, some of the oil wells produced one thousand barrels a day.

In 1906 the town of Owasso was incorporated under the laws of Indian Territory, largely due to efforts by Dr. J. W. Kirksey. Jack Foster was the first mayor and Sam Gideon was the first marshal.

After statehood in 1907, Owasso progressed economically. Voters approved a $20,000 bond issue to build a new brick schoolhouse, completed in 1911. Dan Setser was the first principal of what became known as the Owasso Consolidated Schools.

The population of Owasso remained at only a few hundred people until the end of World War II. Many veterans found jobs in new aircraft industries at the Tulsa International Airport and moved their families into the city limits of Owasso. Land developers, who saw a chance for the town to grow when aerospace industries took off in the 1950s, helped shape the city in north Tulsa County to what it is today, a growing suburb. Owasso was chartered as a city on September 28, 1972.

In the 1990s, Owasso became the state's fastest growing city. The city's estimated population was twenty-nine thousand in 2001. The Cherokee Industrial Park provided hundreds of jobs. Industrial and manufacturing businesses in the park include Bama Pie, Laufin International Tile, The Nordam Group, Ryerson Steel, Sabre, Whirlpool, and WorldCom

RED FORK

In 1884, James Parkinson built a large general store on the Frisco Railroad eighteen miles from the junction of the Cimarron, known as the Red Fork, and Arkansas Rivers. The station became known as Red Fork and was for several years the western terminus of the Frisco in Indian Territory. Red Fork was an important shipping point for cattle raised in the Chickasaw Nation, the Shawnee country, and territory occupied by the Sac and Fox tribes. A post office was established at Red Fork on January 3, 1884.

South and west of Red Fork was unsettled country. The Dalton gang and other outlaws frequented the area. The Daltons once raided H. C. Hall's store at Red Fork.

Red Fork was a sleepy village of about 75 people in 1901 when oil was discovered on an allotment owned by Sue Davis Bland. The new shallow oil field attracted great attention. Within a few months, the population of Red Fork exploded to 1,500.

Red Fork was incorporated in 1902 with an original townsite of 160 acres. Nice homes began to replace crude shacks where oil prospectors had lived. O. B. Jones began a weekly newspaper, Red Fork Derrick. A Presbyterian church housed the town's first school.

Red Fork's growth was stunted when the Frisco Railroad extended its line farther west. With the establishment of Sapulpa, cattle shipments and trade were diverted from Red Fork. With the oil strike at Glenn Pool, oil men left Red Fork, leaving the town with only three hundred inhabitants.

The cowboys and oil field workers who lived in Red Fork gave it a rough a rowdy reputation that lingered for decades. Known as one of Tulsa County's safest areas, legend has it that Red Fork residents like for outsiders to believe its old reputation—it keeps outsiders from moving in.

In 1918, new life was breathed into Red Fork when the Tulsa-Sapulpa Interurban line was built. Workers at large industrial plants in west Tulsa saw Red Fork as a good place to live. Soon, Red Fork had an accredited high school, an active chamber of commerce, and had grown to a thriving city of 2,000 people.

The Red Fork post office was closed on July 31, 1928, after the community was annexed to the City of Tulsa. The post office became the Red Fork Station Tulsa's post office.

Little remains of what became a booming cattle shipping point and oil boom town. Lookout Mountain, known by old-timers as Red Fork Mountain, looms over the original downtown area of Red Fork. A stretch of Interstate 244, built in the 1970s, splits in half the old Red Fork business district.

BIXBY

The first settlement in the area that became Bixby was in 1828. In the early 1890s, an 80-acre townsite was laid out by the government on the Muskogee-Red Fork Trail 15 miles southeast of Tulsa. The location was named Bixby in honor of Tams Bixby, a member of the Dawes Commission. The rich farmland in the area attracted farmers. However, the country was an open range, inhabited by lawless gangs such as the Dalton brothers, the Buck gang, and outlaw Al Jennings.

Some of the outlaws operated from the Spike S Ranch three miles south of the original townsite. In 1900, United States marshals captured Rufus Buck and three members of his gang in a running gun battle south of Bixby.

The Bixby post office was established on July 6, 1899. Bixby's first business was the Turner Mercantile Company that moved to the new townsite from Posey, on Posey Creek, two and a half miles away. The second business in town was a hardware store owned by Jason Best. M. E. Sharp and his son, Harry, opened the Farmers and Merchants Bank in 1901. J. F. Paulter opened the Bank of Bixby the following year.

The first school in Bixby was taught by Alex Williams in a log cabin located on the south side of the townsite. Eliza McGuire gave the land for the school, which was also used by itinerant preachers of several denominations.

✧

A newly developed pepper harvester is demonstrated on a field of fertile cropland near Bixby in 1978.

COURTESY OF THE OKLAHOMA PUBLISHING COMPANY.

Bixby's population in 1900 was twenty-five. As new residents moved into the town, citizens hauled lumber from Sapulpa for the construction of a permanent school. When the Midland Valley Railroad was completed in 1904, old Bixby was moved to its present site in what was known as the Midland Valley Addition, located on the railroad one quarter mile from the Arkansas River. The post office and commercial buildings were moved to the new location.

In 1905, publication of the *Bixby Bulletin* began. Sam Owens owned a ferry boat that took people and vehicles across the Arkansas River. In 1906, the town of Bixby was incorporated with a population of about four hundred. Fred Farr was the first mayor and John Severns the first marshal.

Swampy land around Bixby became rich, productive farmland on both sides of the Arkansas River. Bixby billed itself as the "Garden Spot of Oklahoma." Three elevators stored grain crops harvested by local farmers. In 1909, a 2,280-foot bridge was built across the Arkansas River, connecting ends of the Albert Pike Highway.

Cotton was a major crop around Bixby in the early 1900s. However, by World War I, beans, tomatoes, corn, lettuce, and melons became primary agricultural products. Bixby's

sweet corn is known throughout the region. The annual Green Corn Festival, founded during World War II, is held during corn harvest season. Bixby farmers have also developed the Bixby gold sweet potato.

Bixby remained a farming community until the 1960s when residential development began. Bixby became an official city in 1979.

COLLINSVILLE

A small group of pioneers founded the community that became Collinsville in 1888. In wild and unsettled territory in extreme northeast Tulsa County, coal mines offered jobs to men who wanted them. The coal had to be hauled overland to Oologah to connect with the railroad, but settlers knew the Santa Fe was building south from Kansas and they wanted to be ready for the arrival of the railroad.

Dr. R. E. Graham owned the original eighty-acre townsite laid out by the Dawes Commission. The first post office was opened on May 26, 1897, as Collins, named for Dr. A. Collins, an early surveyor, even though another account attributes the town's name to Dr. A. H. Collins, who owned the post office at present-day Owasso. This second account says that local residents named the new town for

❖

Paula Allen Randolph leads a horse ridden by eight-year-old Kenny Hemm of Tulsa at the Allen Ranch near Bixby.

Dr. Collins after he agreed to move the post office north to the community. Charlie Taylor was the first mayor of Collins that changed its name to Collinsville on June 16, 1898.

When the railroad did come, it missed the original townsite by one mile. The town incorporated and moved to the railroad in the fall of 1899 onto land originally allotted to Thad Morris. Some of the buildings were transported on rollers across a field to Collinsville's present location.

W. L. Wright hauled printing equipment from Oologah to Collinsville and established a weekly newspaper. The first edition of the *Collinsville News* was published on May 11, 1899. When the family newspaper was sold in 1987, it was the oldest newspaper in Tulsa County. The first business in town was a general store owned by W. B. Erwin.

In the early 1900s, gas was discovered in the Collinsville area. The Henry Oil and Gas Company drilled the first well, signaling years of prosperity for the citizens of the community. Large quantities of coal were taken from shallow pits around Collinsville in the first decades of the twentieth century. At its height, more than two hundred tons of coal were shipped from the area each day.

The abundance of inexpensive fuel attracted the Coffeyville Vitrified Brick Company to Collinsville. The company built one of the largest brick plants in the state. In 1911, the Bartlesville Zinc Company built the world's largest zinc smelter in Collinsville.

In addition to industrial development, the farm land around Collinsville produced bumper crops of oats and wheat. Two grain elevators were built to store the grain.

In 1915, the Carnegie Library was built at a cost of $20,000. The following year, Solomon Bayouth opened his first department store in Collinsville. The family-owned business later expanded to Skiatook, Jenks, and Sapulpa.

In 1918, Collinsville voters were asked to consider the transfer of the Collinsville Industrial District to Tulsa County. The area had been part of Rogers County since statehood, but citizens of the town wanted to be part of Tulsa County. On August 24, 1918, voters overwhelmingly approved the annexation to Tulsa County, 1,828 to 8. The

✧
The old train depot in Collinsville now houses the Collinsville Depot Museum, with its displays of early twentieth century home and mission-style furniture.

change added nine thousand residents to the population of Tulsa County and greatly increased the Tulsa County property tax rolls.

Tulsa's Advertising Club welcomed approximately 150 of the new county citizens at a banquet at the Hotel Tulsa in September, 1918. The Collinsville residents were driven to the county fair after arriving by train. A local newspaper reported, "At noon as the train bearing the Collinsville delegation drew into the Frisco depot, the city band broke forth into jubilation and the welcome…followed."

SPERRY

A flag station was established on the present site of Sperry during the completion of the northern section of the Midland Valley Railroad at about the time oil was found in the Bird Creek oil field. The railroad station was called Buehler for Charles Buehler, an official of the Creek and Indiana Oil Company.

The post office was established on May 17, 1902, in a ranch house on Hominy Creek. When R. R. Martin became the postmaster and opened a grocery store near the Buehler station in 1907, the post office was moved, and Buehler became Sperry.

Among the oil speculators drawn to the Bird Creek field was Henry Spybuck, who built the first residential dwelling in Sperry.

Later, Spybuck's son-in-law, Dick Tinker, converted the house into the Tinker Hotel. The origin of Sperry's name is unclear. One story is that it is an Anglicized version of Henry Spybuck's name.

The first free public school in Sperry opened in a two-story brick building in 1911. In 1913, J. D. Winters established the State Guaranty Bank in a one-room frame building.

Sperry was incorporated on March 3, 1917. A. L. Buck was the first mayor. Howard Wickersham the first marshal.

Sperry was filled with roustabouts and roughnecks after the oil strike. However, agriculture was also big business. There were many cattle ranches and cotton farms in the area.

In the twenty-first century, Sperry remains a preserved piece of Americana. Century old brick store fronts line Main Street. The town's unique appearance has attracted the attention of filmmakers. Parts of the town were used in Francis Ford Coppola's movie, *The Outsiders.*

TURLEY

Turley is one of Oklahoma's oldest communities. The settlement sprang up during cattle drive days in 1834. The first town of Turley was located one mile north and one mile east of the present town. A post office in the community, five miles north of Tulsa, opened on January 13, 1897. The town was named for James Turley, co-owner of a general store. Turley was bought out by his partner, A. L. Daum, who served as the postmaster until his death in 1903.

When rumors circulated that the Midland Valley Railroad would be built nearby, Daum's store and post office were moved to a location one half mile north of present Turley. When the railroad was completed, H. L. Buck relocated the town to its present site.

The thirty-acre townsite was platted in 1906 by Manuel Hirsch and H. F. Abby of the Turley Improvement Company. The Turley Lumber Company built the first commercial building. A general store and a blacksmith shop moved from the town's former location. A two-story school was built in 1907 at what is now Sixtieth Street and North Peoria Avenue.

Excellent farmland had attracted original settlers of Turley, but soon farming gave way to the oil industry. The town was in the heart of the Bird Creek field. The first well, a dry hole, was drilled on Delaware Creek northwest of Turley.

The first permanent school house in Turley was a one-room brick building constructed in 1908. As new residents arrived, the school was replaced in 1912 by a four-room brick building.

The Turley post office remained opened until August 23, 1957, when it was consolidated with the Tulsa post office.

❖

Collinsville's Main Street in 1990.

✧

Above: A new city hall in Jenks was completed in 1985.

Below: Jenks' Main Street is a treasure trove of antique shops in storefronts where merchants once sold their wares. Jenks residents proudly call their city "Jenks America."

The unincorporated area continues to celebrate its heritage with the annual Turley Heritage Day's festivities. Because Turley is located in the southwest corner of the Cherokee Nation, Cherokee heritage plays a large part in community pride.

JENKS

The Illinois Townsite Company platted 141 acres as the town of Jenks in February, 1906. The town, located nine miles south of Tulsa on the Midland Valley Railroad, was named for Elmer E. Jenks, an official of the railway.

Most of the early residences in Jenks were built by the Carter Lumber Company that operated under the banner, "The Man Who Thinks Invests in Jenks." The first businesses in the town were the Jenks Café, a rooming house, and a general store. The post office was established January 31, 1905.

In 1906, the Jenks Bank opened and the first grist mill and a general store owned by N. M. Phillips opened for business. In 1912, a bridge constructed across the Arkansas River allowed direct access to Tulsa.

In 1985, the city created the popular downtown antique district that set appearance guidelines, maintaining the image wanted by city fathers.

Jenks' latest attraction is the Oklahoma Aquarium, located on the banks of the Arkansas River. The aquarium, with major theme galleries with hundreds of exhibits, recreates the story of a drop of water that makes the two-thousand-mile journey from the origin of the Arkansas River in Colorado to the Gulf of Mexico.

LEONARD

In the extreme southeastern corner of Tulsa County is the town of Leonard, established in

January 1907, by E. L. Reynolds. A post office opened on August 22, 1908. The town was named for Tulsa banker Oliver H. Leonard.

Leonard became an important shipping point on the Midland Valley Railroad because it was surrounded by oil fields. The town is adjacent to the Wealaka Indian Mission and near the former home of Pleasant Porter, former principal chief of the Creek Nation.

GLENPOOL

Glenpool is known as the town that made Tulsa famous. The town was named for Ida Berryhill Glenn, Creek owner of the land on which oil was discovered in 1905. The oil boom that followed made Tulsa the "Oil Capital of the World." Workers lived in tents and row houses built along present-day U.S. 75 south from 141st Street.

The population of the area around Glenpool grew from 12 families in 1901 to 3,000 residents in 1907. The village changed its name from Glenn Pool to Glenpool with the building of a post office and school in 1908. There is confusion why the town spelled its name differently than the oil field. Over the years, residents have used both spellings.

The Glenn Pool field produced an estimated three hundred million barrels of oil, becoming the nation's richest source of petroleum in the five years following the oil strike. Major oil companies built pipelines from Glenn Pool to refineries in Texas, Kansas, and Illinois.

When oil was discovered at Glenn Pool, leaders in Tulsa seized the moment. Tulsa had the infrastructure of hotels and a railroad, so Glenn Pool never grew beyond the size of an oilfield town.

After the Great Depression, Glenpool once again became a quiet farming town with a population of about six hundred. For years, one general store and a service station were the town's main businesses.

In the mid-1970s, a local engineer, George Gould, installed a modern sewage treatment plant, followed by paved streets, residential development, and utility service lines.

Glenpool incorporated in 1979. The town's population grew from 800 to 2,800 in the 1970s as Tulsans began moving into the suburbs. The oil boom of the early 1980s gave new life to the growing community.

❖

This conveyer line is part of a tissue machine inside the Kimberly-Clark plant in Jenks that stands four stories high.

COURTESY OF THE OKLAHOMA PUBLISHING COMPANY.

CITIES AND TOWNS IN TULSA COUNTY

(2003 Population Estimates from the United States Census Bureau.)

Tulsa County	570,313
Broken Arrow	83,607
Bixby	16,661
Collinsville	4,263
Glenpool	8,407
Jenks	11,560
Lotsee	11
Mannford	2,217
Owasso	21,634
Sand Springs	17,695
Skiatook	5,879
Sperry	1,058
Tulsa	387,807

✧

A 2004 map of the cities and towns of Tulsa County.

COURTESY OF THE OKLAHOMA DEPARTMENT OF TRANSPORTATION.

QUICK FACTS ABOUT TULSA COUNTY'S PEOPLE

Estimated population in 2003 — 570,313
2000 official census — 563,299
1990 — 503,341
1970 — 401,663
1960 — 346,038
1920 — 109,023
1910 — 34,995

From 2000 census —
- 75 % Caucasian; 10.9 % African American; 6.0 % Hispanic; 5.2 % American Indian
- Of citizens over 25, 85 % were high school graduates and 27 % had at least a bachelor's degree from college.

In 2001 —
- 328,130 non-farm workers in 38,400 businesses

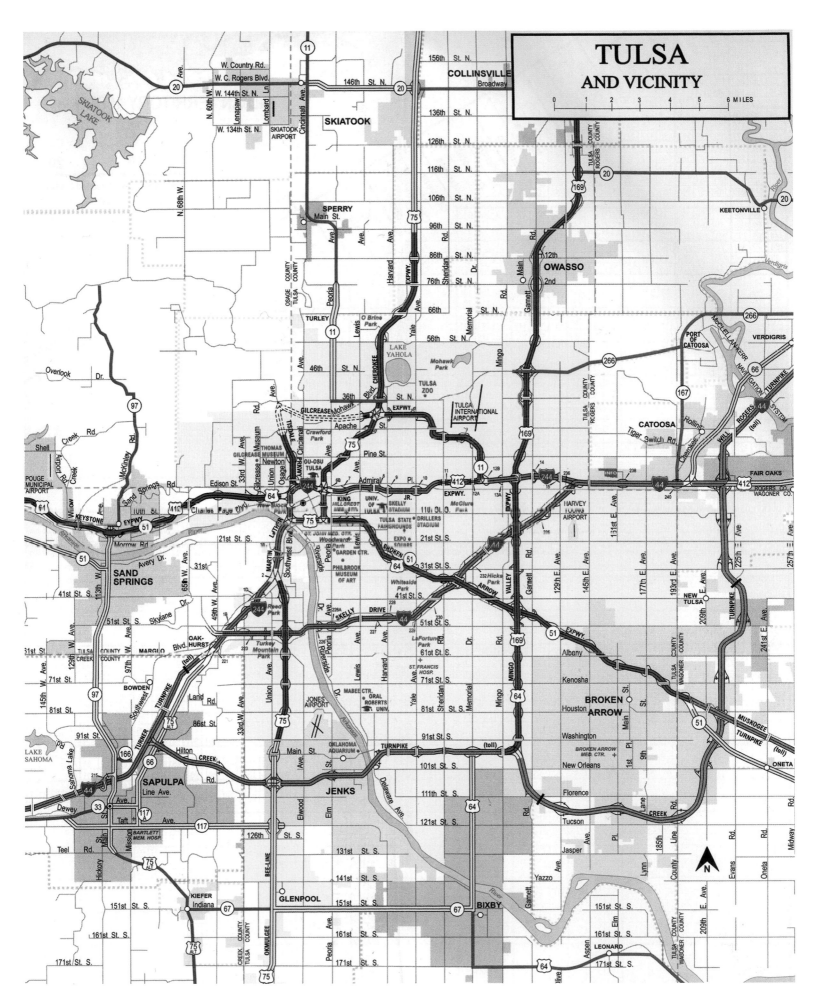

TULSA
AND VICINITY

BIBLIOGRAPHY & SUGGESTED READING

Blakey, Ellen S. *Tulsa Spirit*. Tulsa: Continental Heritage Press, 1979.

Brossard, E. B. *Petroleum, Politics and Power*. Tulsa: PennWell Books, 1983.

Butler, William. *Tulsa 75: A History of Tulsa, Oklahoma*. Tulsa: The Metropolitan Tulsa Chamber of Commerce, 1974.

Clinton, Fred. *First Oil and Gas Well in Tulsa County*. Oklahoma City: Oklahoma Historical Society, 1952.

Connelly, W. L. *The Oil Business as I Saw It*. Norman: University of Oklahoma Press, 1954.

Debo, Angie. *Tulsa: From Creek Town to Oil Capital*. Norman: University of Oklahoma Press, 1943.

Douglas, Clarence B. *The History of Tulsa*. 3 volumes. Chicago: Clarke Press, 1921.

Duncan, Jean. *A Patchbook of Memories*. Tulsa: J.R. Woods, 1983.

Dunn, Nina Lane. *Tulsa's Magic Roots*. Tulsa: Oklahoma Book Publishing Company, 1979.

Everly-Douze, Susan. *Tulsa Times: A Pictorial History: The Boom Years*. Tulsa: World Publishing Company, 1987.

_____. *Tulsa Times: A Pictorial History: Coming of Age*. Tulsa: World Publishing Company, 1988.

_____. *Tulsa: A Pictorial History: The Early Years*. Tulsa: World Publishing Company, 1986.

Federal Writers Project: *Tulsa: A Guide to the Oil Capital*. Tulsa: Mid-West Printing Co., 1938.

Franks, Clyda. *Tulsa: Where the Streets Were Paved With Gold*. Chicago: Arcadia Publishing, 2000.

Franks, Kenny A. *The Oklahoma Petroleum Industry*. Norman: University of Oklahoma Press, 1980.

Gates, Eddie Faye. *Riot on Greenwood: The Total Destruction of Black Wall Street*. Austin, Texas: Sunbelt Eakin, 2003.

Goble, Danney. *Tulsa! Biography of the American City*. Tulsa: Council Oak Books, 1997.

Hamill, John. *Tulsa: The Great American City*. Montgomery, Alabama: Community Communications, Inc., 2000.

Herndon, V. E. *The Story of Tulsa: From an Indian Village to a Modern Metropolis*. Tulsa: Tulsa Public Schools, 1950.

Inhofe, Marilyn. *Footsteps through Tulsa*. Tulsa: Inhofe, Reeves, Jones, 1984.

Landis, Jamye K. *Sand Springs, Oklahoma*. Chicago: Arcadia Publishing, 1999.

Lee, Victoria. "Movers and Shakers." Tulsa: A Touch of Heart Publishing, 1997.

Logsdon, William G. *The University of Tulsa*. Norman: Oklahoma Heritage Association, 1977.

McCombs, Wayne. *Let's Goooooooooooo Tulsa! The History and Record Book of Professional Baseball in Tulsa, Oklahoma, 1905-1989*. Tulsa: Self-published, 1990.

Savage, William A. Jr. *Singing Cowboys and All that Jazz*. Norman: University of Oklahoma Press, 1983.

Stapleton, Steven L. *Broken Arrow: The First Hundred Years*. Virginia Beach: Donning Company Publishers, 2002.

✧

The banks of the Arkansas River provide miles of parks and recreational use. In this photograph, a floating stage is readied for use during Oktoberfest.

COURTESY OF THE OKLAHOMA PUBLISHING COMPANY.

CHAPTER VII

85

✧
A Tulsa night from the southwest, 1977.

SHARING THE HERITAGE

historic profiles of businesses,

organizations, and families that

have contributed to the development and

economic base of Tulsa and Tulsa County

SPECIAL
THANKS TO

McGraw, Davisson & Stewart

Ramsey Winch

Turnpike Transit Company

G. C. BROACH

The G. C. Broach Company is a unique, independently owned organization of experienced professionals whose ultimate endeavor is the design and construction of direct-fired process heaters.

The company was founded and incorporated on December 27, 1960, by G. C. "Clayton" Broach on the premise that the dependability and performance of any heater are directly equated to the quality of the engineering techniques employed in the design and construction of the unit. And, that most causes of operational problems and failures should be identified and eliminated in the basic design of the equipment.

Nearing a half-century of successful operation, the company that was started by Clayton and his wife, Louise, is still going strong. Employing seventy to one hundred people at any given time, the G. C. Broach Company has reported annual sales that averaged $8 million to as great as $20 million and boasts a large customer base. Impressive considering that Clayton and Louise, along with their three small children, sold the family home in April of 1960 to finance their new heater company.

G. C. Broach is no stranger to challenge and hard work. Born in October 1928, he went to work in a print shop at age fourteen to help with living expenses for his sister and widowed mother. At age fifteen, he met Louise Cue, the woman who would be his wife only four years later in 1947. He served in the military from 1946 to 1948 and 1950 to 1951 and, in 1954, earned a B.S. in Business Law from the University of Tulsa.

Only six years later, the Broach's rented a two-bedroom home for $75 a month, while Clayton ran his fledgling company from a glassed-in back porch. One year later, the G. C. Broach Company was large enough to begin renting office space near downtown Tulsa at Fifth and Peoria.

By the mid-1960s, the G. C. Broach Company became a major supplier of Refinery, Gas Plant and Oil Production Heaters. In 1965 a fabrication shop was built in Tulsa to allow the company to offer a completely in-house turnkey project. An additional location was also opened that year in Paris, France. After a five-year run, Broach Paris was closed after it was decided to centralize all operations to its Tulsa offices.

Broach's manufacturing complex was designed and built exclusively for the construction of process heaters. Located on fifteen acres, the plant is served by the Union Pacific Railroad via the company's three private rail spurs. A completed unit can be withdrawn from an individual assembly bay door onto a track mounted transfer car, which is aligned with a rail spur and the unit is

✧

Above: Clayton Broach with three of his four sons.

Below: Clayton Broach on his four-wheeler at his yearly farm party.

withdrawn from the transfer car onto the rail car. The shop floor and the transfer car are both rail car height so the unit does not have to be lifted for loading. This system minimizes the possibility of any damage to a unit during loading and affects a net saving to the customer by eliminating expensive lifting costs.

The company's central geographic location in mid-America gives quick, easy access to all parts of the nation and the world with transportation choices ranging from rail, truck or barge transportation. One of the unique features of the facility is that all manufacturing functions are performed under

one roof, in environmentally controlled conditions, so that weather is not a factor in scheduling. Consistent, thermostatically controlled temperatures and uniform lighting are maintained throughout to provide year-round control of product quality.

In the 1970s the Broach Company extended its design scope of supply by furnishing skid mounted heat medium systems, including pumps, expansion tanks, piping and controls (all fully piped, wired and shop tested). The Adjunct Loop Air Preheat system was developed and patented in nine countries by GCB during this period. With this system, the oil is circulated through a convection coil in the top of the heater to absorb heat that would normally be wasted into the atmosphere. After absorbing this heat, the oil is circulated through an exchanger in the combustion air stream to heat the combustion air, thereby putting the otherwise wasted heat back into the furnace. To this day, the Adjunct Loop proves to be a superior air preheat system.

During 1974 the office location was moved to its

Above: Aerial view of Broach's 84,000 square foot plant facility.

Below: Broach Corporate Office at 7667 East Forty-sixth Place in Tulsa.

current address at 7667 East Forty-sixth Place. After this move, sons Christopher C. and Brian R. Broach joined the company and are currently officers of the company. Christopher will celebrate thirty years of service since graduating with a B.S. in Chemical Engineering from the University of Tulsa in 1979 and Brian will celebrate thirty-one years with an extensive background in Mechanical, Chemical, Thermal and Petroleum Engineering.

emerged from Broach during those years include the EZ Mount Light Pole, which is a prefabricated stationary or removable pole that is used on walkways and docks in industrial locations. Another design was a Lean/Master Lead/Lag Transmitter that provides the Lead/Lag function in forced draft combustion systems, providing the best approach to prevent combustion upsets during load swings.

The 1980s became known as the "Death Valley Days" for the industry as a whole. Oil prices soared, production plummeted and heater businesses began to fail. Additionally, the 1980s marked a shift to process heaters that required a higher degree of engineering and emissions control. Some special designs and innovations that

In 1984, Broach took a gamble on a large project with All-American Pipeline which was building a pipeline that required thirty-five heaters from Los Angeles, California to Baytown, Texas. The project was enormous and the possibility of winning the project was remote. Nonetheless, Broach committed personnel to work on it for over a year

without a promise of an award. It was affectionately called the "Kite in the Wind" project; Broach won the project on Valentine's Day, 1985. It was the largest single order for a process heater company given during those "Death Valley" years. They were able to keep local vendors alive when no one else was busy.

A third son, Roger C. Broach, vice president, joined the company during these years after earning a B.S. in Business Administration in 1987 from Oklahoma State University.

Although the 1990s were prosperous for the company, a veil of melancholy lay over the daily activities due to Louise Broach's death in July of 1990 after a brief struggle with cancer.

Today, The G.C. Broach Company continues to look ahead by implementing a strategic business plan. The company's goals include:

- Striving for innovation toward quality, design, and improvements of their products;
- Being thorough and complete with their designs and contracts in order to preserve customer satisfaction while optimizing costs while maintaining, or improving, quality and service to their customers;
- Maintaining a debt-free operation and keeping cash, or equivalent, on hand so that the cyclic downturns characteristic of the business don't bring upset;
- Paying vendors on or before invoice due dates in order to preserve the good, quick service provided by those vendors and to maintain an impeccable credit rating; and
- Striving to give back to the community which gives The G.C. Broach Company so much, they participate with Executive Women International, the Philbrook and Gilcrease Museums, Boy Scouts of America, American Cancer Society and Up with Trees.

✧

Above: All American Pipeline heaters under construction.

Bottom: Hot Oil Heater operating at ninety-five percent efficiency with Broach Adjunct Loop.

RENAISSANCE TULSA HOTEL & CONVENTION CENTER

In February 2003, John Q. Hammons unveiled the city's first full service hotel since 1984 at 6808 South 107th East Avenue in Tulsa—the Renaissance Tulsa Hotel & Convention Center by Marriott. Providing traditional service to a contemporary clientele, the hotel offers an elegant European style marked by exquisite restaurant and lounge dining, comfortable and well-appointed "Rooms that Work" guest rooms.

The luxurious complex at U.S. 169 and Seventy-first Street offers guests over fifty thousand square feet of meeting space and is Tulsa's only AAA-rated Four Diamond award-winning hotel. A prime location for business or pleasure, the Renaissance Tulsa is located in an area that serves as Tulsa's shopping and dining corridor including the Woodland Hills Mall and the new East Market Shopping Center. Located only ten miles south of Tulsa International Airport it is easily accessible from Highway 169 and the Creek Turnpike.

The hotel's principal owner and developer, John Q. Hammons Hotels, Inc., has been the nation's leading independent builder, developer, owner and manager of upscale, full-service hotels, resorts and suites since its inception in 1958. Based in Springfield, Missouri, the company operates properties nationwide under the following brands: Embassy Suites Hotels, Renaissance, Marriott, Radisson, Residence Inn, Homewood Suites by Hilton, Holiday Inn and Courtyard by Marriott.

Founder and industry icon John Q. Hammons' historic leadership has made the Renaissance name synonymous with luxury accommodations, elegant dining, and spacious meeting facilities in cities across the country. Renowned as a philanthropist and visionary, Hammons has secured a number of high-profile events hosted by Renaissance Tulsa. They include 2004's Henry P. Iba Citizen Athlete Awards honoring such sports

figures as Ozzie Smith, Jackie Joyner Kersee, and John Wooden, and the annual John Q. Hammons Hotel Classic has quickly become an elite tournament stop along the LPGA Tour. Hammons also partnered with Tulsa's own Union High School to build the impressive John Q. Hammons Arena at the Union Multipurpose Activity Center, complete with professionally crafted portable wood flooring and extensive seating space for students.

The Renaissance Tulsa Hotel & Convention Center is home to the State of Oklahoma's largest ballroom, the beautiful 28,800-square-foot Renaissance Grand Ballroom, the 7,200-square-foot Madrid Ballroom, and the 3,600-square-foot Seville Ballroom. Nine additional meeting rooms including three boardrooms and four hospitality suites are provided with state-of-the-art audio visual and video conferencing capabilities, high speed and direct Internet access, and convenient complimentary self parking. Full- and self-service business centers are also available on site.

Hotel accommodations include 300 spacious and elegant guest rooms, 64 with balconies and 36 suites. Standard amenities in every room include voice mail, high-speed Internet access, data ports, task lighting, work desk and chair, comfortable reading/relaxation chair, down duvet, seven-inch foam mattress with quilted top, hairdryers, Bath & Body Works amenities, complimentary in-room coffee and tea service, iron and ironing board, in-room safe, and twenty-seven inch cable/satellite televisions with remote control and in-room movies. The Renaissance's Club Level is available with complimentary continental breakfast and nightly appetizers, a club lounge with concierge, two robes and turndown services. Suites include additional living areas with a television, queen sleeper sofa, wet bar, mini refrigerator, microwave and two robes.

The award winning hotel restaurant, Cyprus Grille, serves breakfast, lunch and dinner daily, while elegant evening dining includes exceptional steaks and seafood with a Mediterranean flair, as well as breakfast buffets and other offerings from an extensive menu. The Renaissance's Merlots Wine Bar and Lounge is open every day for light fare and a selection of wines by the glass. Room service is also available.

For recreation, guests can enjoy an on-site fitness center, relax in the heated indoor pool with sauna and whirlpool, or truly unwind in the hotel's day spa. Golf enthusiasts will appreciate six award-winning courses located within a ten-mile radius of the hotel. Tulsa's

enormous variety of cultural activities includes the Oklahoma Aquarium, Brady Theater District, Philbrook and Gilcrease Art Museums, and the Tulsa State Fairgrounds—and all within a reasonable distance from the hotel.

Complimentary on-site parking is always available at the Renaissance Tulsa Hotel & Convention Center and valet parking is available at ten dollars per day. Pets are allowed with some restrictions and a refundable deposit.

Celebrating the historic essence of Tulsa and its unique relationship to the hotel, one writer welcomed future guests with these inspired words, "Those preceding you had the spirit. And Tulsa shows it to this day: the restless ambition, the wild optimism of its oil barons. Cloaked in European artistic instincts and rooted

in New World possibilities, those visionaries set about to establish the style that is distinctively Tulsa. It remains a style that refreshes the sensibilities, elegantly expressed in the unique personality of The Renaissance Tulsa Hotel & Convention Center, from the moment you cross the threshold into the grand lobby, greeted by the savvy service of our bell staff, you engage the essence of comforts. If not lured first by the inspired cuisine of our highly acclaimed Cyprus Grille, you will find yourself reinvigorated by our spacious and abundantly appointed guest rooms. Like the barons of old, you will be captivated by the luxury that surrounds your stay with us. We welcome you."

For more information and to make reservations at the Renaissance Tulsa Hotel & Convention Center, call toll-free 1-800-264-0165 or 918-307-2600, or visit www.renaisssncetulsa.com.

Tommy and Lucille Day founded the Daylight Donut Flour business in 1954 in Tulsa. They produced their famous light donut mix each morning and sold it to shops in the afternoon, most often from the trunk of their car. Thus, "Day" was derived from the last name of the founders and "Light" described the texture and flavor of the donuts the flour produced.

By the end of their fifth year, sales had dramatically increased and two additional employees were hired. The Days retired in 1977, selling their company to Jerry and Linda Hull of Tulsa. The Hulls introduced more new products, a complete line of donut making equipment, a new facility, and a fleet of tractor-trailer delivery trucks. By then the business had grown to over two hundred Daylight Donut shops. The first international Daylight Donut store opened in 1990 and now includes sixty-five other stores in Mexico, Austria, Guatemala, Romania, Greece, Japan, Saudi Arabia, and Bolivia.

In January 2002, John and Sheila Bond bought the Daylight Corporation from the Hulls. John and Sheila joined the Daylight organization in 1977 as owners and operators of their first daylight donut shop in Oklahoma, later adding two additional shops to their roster. In 1987 the Bonds sold their shops and John went to work for the Daylight Corporation as a sales representative. In 1989 he became a sales coordinator and in 1990, was named vice president of sales. In 1992 he was promoted to vice president and CEO and, in 1995, assumed the responsibilities and title of president and CEO.

Today, Daylight occupies a sixty-five-thousand-square-foot warehouse and manufacturing facility. The site is state-of-the-art in sanitation, efficiency, and consistency of quality products, and is complimented by two office complexes. A new fleet of tractor-trailer trucks deliver mix and supplies to the Daylight Donut shops from coast to coast. International shipments are made over land to ports and then sent by ship to foreign destinations. The equipment arm of Daylight Corporation has expanded with the most modern technology in producing efficient quality equipment to manufacture Daylight Donuts at the lowest costs.

The owners of Daylight Donut shops come from various occupations—teachers, personnel managers, engineers, and doctors. The Daylight Corporation supplies over 500 Daylight Donut shops both domestic and international. During the year 2000, Daylight opened seventy-two new Daylight Donut shops. This growth is due, in part, to the fact that shop owners pay no franchise fees, no royalties, and no hidden costs.

Still located at 11707 East Eleventh Street in Tulsa, the philosophy of Daylight's founders holds true in the twenty-first century: "Through hard work and the entrepreneurial spirit you can capture your dreams." For more information about the company, its merchandise, and opportunities for opening a Daylight Donut Store, please visit www.daylightdonuts.com.

❖

Below: A bird's eye view of the Daylight Corporation's international headquarters at 11707 East Eleventh Street in Tulsa.

Bottom: Tractor-trailer trucks are loaded with Daylight's famous mix and supplies for shipment all across the country.

MPSI Systems

Ron Harper founded MPSI in 1970, and from the beginning, the story has been one of vision and determination. Working from a small room in his Tulsa home, Harper started out with $500 in working capital and no tangible product to sell. Not a promising start, or so it would seem. What Harper did possess was a concept of a computer model, which he had started as a ten-hour research project while working on his MBA at the University of Kansas. The computer model was designed to help petroleum marketers select the most profitable sites for their outlets.

Harper landed his first contract with Skelly Oil—later Getty Oil—in Tulsa less than one year after launching the company. Looking for a better way to select locations for its retail gasoline outlets, Skelly turned to the one-man MPSI operation for help in evaluating six local Skelly outlets.

Five of the outlets were under construction and one had already been branded a "loser" and closed. Using his statistical site selection model, Harper told Skelly that all five of the outlets under construction would fail. Within six months, the prediction came true. Harper also told Skelly that the outlet it had closed was not a failure and if converted to a self-serve gasoline outlet, it would succeed. The conversion was made and the outlet became a success for both Skelly Oil and Tulsa, becoming the area's first self-serve outlet. Skelly

officials, who then recommended MPSI to other oil companies, deemed the overall project a total success.

With a growing number of oil companies realizing the value of MPSI's site selection model, the early 1970s proved to be a time of growth for the company. Sales increased and the employee base expanded. For MPSI, the future looked promising. Then, the unexpected happened.

In 1973, the Middle East oil embargo hit. At the time, MPSI's main product was the site selection model and its only clients were U.S. oil companies. The oil embargo severely cut crude exports, sending prices skyrocketing and shaking the overall economy. With controls limiting petroleum allotment to existing sites only, U.S. oil companies were forced to stop building new sites. For MPSI, the result was devastating. It meant that clients no longer needed a site selection model. The company had less than six months of cash and a product with no market.

MPSI quickly responded to the challenge. Realizing that the embargo had not affected every country, the company began

✧

Above: MPSI's mapping capabilities and graphic solution technology placed it at the forefront of the computer graphics industry in the 1980s.

Below: MPSI's corporate office in Tulsa, Oklahoma

selling its site selection model to oil companies in Canada. The success of that decision became the starting point for international expansion. MPSI also made another important decision—to diversify its business into other industries, lessening its dependence on the petroleum industry.

The company's two-fold strategy paid off. By 1980, MPSI had evaluated over 130,000 retail locations throughout the U.S., U.K., Canada, Australia, France, Sweden, Germany, Holland and Switzerland. It was also successfully doing business in a variety of retail environments, including the petroleum, banking, convenience food and restaurant industries. 1980 was also a landmark year for another reason. MPSI expanded the use of its system from site selection to a system capable of evaluating many facets of the retail planning process. It took three years and all of the research dollars it had to expand the system, but once completed, the company grew dramatically. In 1983, MPSI became a public company. And by 1989, geographic expansion had increased to fifty-seven countries and company revenues were at an all time high.

The success of the 1980s was quickly challenged by the roller-coaster years of the next decade. Ushering in the 1990s was a sluggish worldwide economy showing slow sales across the retail landscape. New technologies were bombarding the market and MPSI's customers were rapidly redefining their product requirements. Unprecedented mergers of major global oil giants, thereby reducing the traditional sales targets for MPSI, also characterized this period. In response, MPSI streamlined its workforce and production methods, developed a new generation of software and decision support services and expanded its retail consulting capabilities. By 1995, MPSI had dramatically reduced operating costs and increased profits, and by the end of the decade, it had established a major presence in eighty countries.

The new millennium was a time of repositioning for MPSI. The company began aggressively marketing its retail data warehouse through new sales channels, and launched

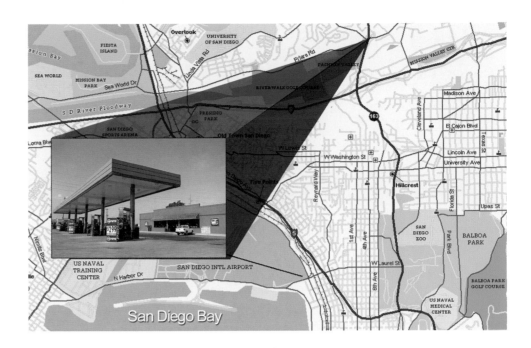

comprehensive online analysis and retail data tools. One of the most significant changes took place in August 2004 when company shareholders voted to take MPSI private in an effort to reduce the escalating costs of operating as a public company.

Although, still one of the world's most recognized site selection providers, today MPSI offers a host of retail data and marketing solutions. The company has more than 400 customers in over 85 countries, ranging from top Fortune 500 companies owning thousands of retail sites to retailers with one location. MPSI's customer base includes nearly half of the top twenty Fortune 500 companies. MPSI continues to be headquartered in Tulsa, Oklahoma, while also maintaining support offices around the world.

✧

MPSI's decision support systems assist retailers in more than eighty-five countries.

THE HOLMES ORGANISATION

Choosing the right insurance partner is easy—just find an experienced agency with the ability to focus on your specific needs.

Since 1963 that choice has been The Holmes Organisation, one of Tulsa's largest and most respected independent insurance firms. Using well-established relationships with the world's best-known insurance companies, this firm provides a broad range of insurance and risk management services to middle- and upper-tier commercial accounts.

"Our clients are primarily privately held corporations, although we also represent publicly traded companies," said Bill Grant, president of The Holmes Organisation. "The size and industry mix of our clients covers a wide range. Our clients buy, sell, start up, spin off, grow and enter new business ventures and work hard to achieve business success. We work hard with them. The majority of our clients are headquartered in this geographic region, but we have longevity with clients across the United States with assets located worldwide."

Founded in 1963 and headquartered in Tulsa, the company's exceptional reputation and success can be traced to a simple philosophy—constantly add value during the process of providing a customized insurance programs.

The Holmes Organisation has an insurance pedigree that few in the region can match.

Top: The Holmes Organization brings together a talented team of professionals to provide customized insurance programs.

Below: Holmes utilizes the latest technology to provide clients with valuable information.

Burt Holmes, the firm's founder and current board member, began his own company after working more than ten years at the well-respected insurance firm of his father, Dan P. Holmes.

"I started Burt B. Holmes & Associates with one partner and a part-time clerical person," he said. "We were in the general insurance business—property, life, accident and health. We ended up growing at a rate of fifteen to twenty percent a year for many years. When you're small, you can do that."

A factor in this early success no doubt had to do with some of the firm's well-known clients like QuikTrip, which Holmes also helped found. This, combined with his involvement in a variety of local organizations like The University of Tulsa and Gilcrease Museum, provided the kind of visibility that assured the firm a spot among Tulsa's business elite.

And while we're on the topic of visibility—what's in a name? While there are many reasons Tulsans know and appreciate The Holmes Organisation, there's one in particular that has caught their attention and curiosity over the years.

It's the "s."

When Holmes was coming up with the company's new name years ago, he decided to base it on another company that used the British spelling of 'Organisation.'

"I knew it would pique people's interest, and it did. It's been fantastic over the years," he said. "You want people to think about you and remember your name. And they do."

Today the Holmes Organisation staff numbers more than sixty insurance professionals who handle clients' needs in commercial property & casualty, benefits, life, accident & health, estate planning, investment services and personal lines insurance.

Over the years, The Holmes Organisation has built particular knowledge—and established specialized practice groups—in numerous areas, including Risk Management, Energy, Banking, Wholesalers, Real Estate, Refuse Sanitation, Aviation, Law, Equine Insurance, Marine and Manufacturing.

This is an agency that believes "how" it operates is what sets it apart from everyone else. That means many things for this versatile Tulsa firm: customized procedures for implementing clients' programs, monitoring new regulations and legislation that could affect clients from an insurance perspective, even offering a consolidated billing system that saves employers time and money. Because the firm has no allegiance to any specific carrier or vendor, the firm contracts with nearly all the major insurance companies to deliver a wide range of insurance products.

The Holmes Organisation also takes advantage of leading-edge technology to provide its clients with the latest data analysis, legislative and communication tools, laptop and online plan enrollments—even the option of an efficient "paperless" program where all documents are delivered to clients online.

"We possess the information and experience to negotiate comprehensive, competitive benefits programs," said Grant. "We know where to find the answers to any of our clients' insurance, employee benefits and human resources questions."

Joining Grant in helping the company evolve today are Stuart DeSelms and Jeff Holmes, who together bought the firm in 1998 from Burt Holmes and his longtime partner Kent Bogart—and they have been growing the business ever since. Their task is to take the company to new heights in an

insurance industry that is experiencing major changes. To accomplish their goals for the future, The Holmes Organisation is staying ahead of that curve by transitioning to the latest technology and focusing more and more on specific industry "niches" where the firm has built experience.

"We've developed a reputation for being a fun, fair place to work," said Grant. "Because of that, we've had more opportunities to talk to bright young people. We've got people coming to us asking to work here. That number grows more and more."

Some other important numbers tell the story as well: In the past six years, the firm's number of employees has nearly doubled as more people decide they want to work for The Holmes Organisation. In those same six years, the firm's revenues have tripled.

"Most commercial clients realize that the old days of simply selling policies are behind us," explained Grant. "We are continuing to provide tools to control risk at the lowest possible cost. Once that is achieved, then placing the policies almost becomes an afterthought."

There's one final number that tells The Holmes Organisation story: the firm has set a goal for itself to be one of the largest privately held brokers in the country by 2010.

"In order to gain membership in that club," said Grant, "we must constantly add value that is unexpected by our clients."

✧

Above: Holmes Organisation is located at 1350 South Boulder in Tulsa, Oklahoma.

Below: The firm's leadership team includes, (from right to left): Jeff Holmes, Bill Grant, Stuart DeSelms, and Burt Holmes.

Morrow-Gill Lumber Company

Above: Morrow-Gill Lumber Company in 1956.

Below: Morrow-Gill Lumber Company in 2004.

Fifty years of experience and quality service have made Morrow-Gill Lumber Company the last lumberyard in town and changing when necessary while keeping what works has been the company's key to its longevity and continued success in the Tulsa area. In 1954, Dale Morrow, along with Claude Gill, ventured into the world of family-owned business, and today Vicki Sisney, Morrow's daughter, continues to oversee the longtime Sand Springs store and lumberyard as vice president and CEO of the company. She and her three sisters own the company, along with their father. At age ninety-two, Morrow still stops in to wait on customers, sharing his expertise on electrical

and plumbing how-to's. Morrow was honored to receive the John M. Hess Award for Outstanding Citizenship in 2003.

Morrow, a World War II veteran, moved to Sand Springs from Terral, Oklahoma, just South of Duncan, in 1946. After many successful years as co-owner of the Morrow-Gill Lumber Company, in 1993 he bought the lumber company from the Gill family thirty-five years after Gill's death. He also became a prominent resident of the community, serving on the city council from 1963 to 1976 and served honorably as the town's mayor from 1969 to 1972. In 1969, Morrow and other citizens came together to convince city leaders to change a city government that was run by three people to a city council form of government, with a city manager responsible for the city's daily operations. Another achievement of Morrow's tenure as councilor was the adoption of a citywide sales tax as a source of revenue that provided improvement for city streets, water and sewer system and paid for the first police car in Sand Springs.

Vicki literally worked her way up in the company, starting at age four when she would enjoy carefree days at the lumberyard when her parents needed a babysitter. As an older child, she was put to work with a feather duster and given other small tasks but was not

officially on the payroll until 1971 when she took the job held by the retiring bookkeeper. In 2004 she became the first female president of the Oklahoma Lumberman's Association, which consists of nearly 250 lumber retailers and seventy-five vendors. Having worked at the store for so long, Vicki's specialty is behind the scenes, crunching numbers, projecting orders and managing financing.

The company employs nineteen people who "make all the difference in the world," according to Vicki. Most employees have been with the company for ten years or more and are treated with a large dose of tender loving care under her management, including shorter workweeks and establishing a 401K plan. Tom Watson is the store manager and has remained dedicated and well-loved by employees and customers alike throughout his career at the lumber company. Both of Vicki's sons, Chris and Bryan Thomas, also enjoy working in the family-owned company. And although working with family has its quirks, she wouldn't have it any other way.

Though the customer base has dwindled somewhat from the do-it-yourselfers of the past, Vicki has maintained security in the business by courting contractors, realizing they are the key to large building projects. She says, "We have the information, the product and the skills knowledge."

Striving to give back to the community, Vicki and her employees are involved in as many community outreach projects as possible, aiming to give a little back to the city that has given their business so much.

Visitors to the town might mistake the Morrow-Gill Lumber Company for something other than a lumberyard if they visit just as the business opens. "Regulars" will come around and share a cup of coffee, catch up on news, wait out a rain shower, or see what the

price of lumber is doing—pretty much the same thing carpenters and plumbers did fifty years ago, when the business opened. Small-town service, big-time quality...you'll find both at Morrow-Gill Lumber Company at 200 East Morrow Road in Sand Springs.

❖

Above: Dale C. Morrow.

Below: Left to right: Store Manger Tom Watson, Vicki Sisney, and Vicki's oldest son, Bryan Thomas.

RIB CRIB
BBQ & GRILL

❖

Below: Rib Crib's prototype was designed to look like a log cabin. It has 4,000–4,500 square feet with 175 to 200 seats.

Bottom: All Rib Crib interiors have a whimsical western décor.

The world has Bret Chandler to thank for his barbecue restaurant that started in 1992 in an old, remodeled house near the University of Tulsa. Since that time, Rib Crib has expanded to over forty restaurants around the country. With a goal of reaching 100 restaurants in the next five years, Chandler continues to perfect his recipe for success.

Chandler's future was partly paved for him when he graduated in 1983 with a petroleum and land management degree from the University of Oklahoma and found the oil business "had softened a bit." So instead of entering the oil business, he opted for pizza, becoming a Mazzio's franchisee in Florida for five years. In 1988, he started his own construction company, but by 1992, he was ready for something else. For Chandler that meant answering the call of the restaurant industry once again. Many attractions, including the pace, atmosphere and people, but mostly the opportunity to return to Tulsa, drew him to research which kind of restaurant would make it. The niche he found was in barbecue and Chandler set out creating not only unique sauces and rubs and methods for cooking and serving the barbecue but also a method to duplicate what was to become a very successful restaurant. "I wanted to apply the same disciplines—quality, service, cleanliness, and value—to a barbecue concept that other well-established casual dining chains employ," says Chandler.

After remodeling the old home on South Harvard in 1992 and converting restaurant buildings into Rib Cribs through 1997, the first freestanding prototype Rib Crib opened in 1998. Successful openings of the first Rib Cribs outside of Oklahoma in Missouri and Florida in 1999 clearly made franchising a viable expansion strategy and, by 2006, the company included over forty restaurants in seven states and is well on their way to becoming a strong regional and emerging national chain. As testimony to Rib Crib's popularity, Rib Crib has won media accolades for "best barbecue" in many of the towns and cities where it has opened.

Rib Crib's mission statement, "Boldly deliver the highest quality with a passion for excellence" is engrained in their employees from the beginning. Chandler says, "We continually ask ourselves, 'What are we learning and how are we improving?'" Chandler established this thinking from the start. Being a believer in finding good people and letting them make their own decisions, Chandler knows that "employees respond to being empowered and when you attract and retain those people, everyone benefits." The Tulsa Metro Chamber recognized this fundamental model of such a successful business in 2000 when they named Chandler "Entrepreneur of the Year." Rib Crib has also been distinguished many times as one of the fastest growing privately held businesses in Oklahoma.

Chandler is a firm believer in giving back to the communities that support his restaurants.

Rib Crib plays a major role in community organizations such as the March of Dimes, Cystic Fibrosis, local high schools and universities.

For over a decade individuals, families, businesses and organizations have enjoyed Rib Crib's high-quality menu, which includes a wide variety of hickory-smoked meats served in sandwiches, dinners and combination platters. They also offer smoked chicken Caesar salads and wraps, smoked chicken quesadillas and super spuds. Diners will enjoy Rib Crib's full-service, whimsical western-style dining atmosphere or carryout and catering are available. For a complete menu, catering information and list of locations, please visit www.ribcrib.com or call (918) 712-7427.

Top: The CribWich, a Rib Crib original creation of hot links and brisket on a fresh bun.

Middle: Rib Crib's famous Baby Back Ribs.

Bottom: Cool, fresh greens are loaded with our famous golden crispy chicken tenders, diced tomatoes, shredded Cheddar cheese and savory Ranch Dressing. It is crowned with crisp Cheddar tortilla strips for a tangy finish.

AMERISUITES

AmeriSuites Tulsa is located at 7037 South Zurich Avenue and is less than ten miles from many of the city's most popular attractions: Warren Place, Oral Roberts University, Mabee Center, Expo Square, Tulsa Drillers Baseball Stadium, Bell's Amusement Park & Big Splash Water Park, the internationally famous Philbrook Museum, and the unique Oklahoma Aquarium. Tulsa's award-winning zoo and outstanding penguin exhibit, and the Tulsa International Airport are only fifteen miles away. The all-suites hotel's close proximity to other locations such as Woodland Hills Mall, St. Francis Hospital and the University of Tulsa also makes it an appealing destination for travelers from around the world.

Whether traveling on business or pleasure, AmeriSuites Tulsa will fit most any traveler's needs. The 128 suites are beautifully furnished with mini-kitchens offering refrigerators and microwaves, in-room coffee makers, twenty-seven inch televisions wired with cable and access to VCP/CNN/ESPN/HBO and pay-per-view movies, iron, ironing board and hair dryer in the room, free copies of *USA Today* and *Financial Times* and the best reward of all, free nights and airline miles with Prime Rewards™. A fitness center, heated outdoor pool, guest laundry facilities and valet service combined with the free Bountiful

Breakfast Buffet™ make this home away from home appealing to even the most frequent traveler.

Corporate business guests will appreciate the fifty-one TCB (Taking Care of Business) Suites™ available which include special amenities suited just for the business traveler. Two-line speakerphones are available with data ports for guests working on-line and conducting business while they sit at an oversized executive desk with a side desk return on wheels that adjusts to left- or right- handed working needs. A Smart Lamp with additional receptacles for office electronics keeps guests from spending time on the floor searching for electrical outlets. An upholstered executive chair ensures maximum comfort during work-time, while an oversized leisure chair and ottoman with snacks is provided when relaxing is in order.

AmeriSuites Tulsa is backed by Prime Hospitality Corporation (NYSE:PDQ), one of the nation's premiere lodging companies. AmeriSuites is Prime's flagship all-suite brand and has become a favorite of both business and leisure travelers. A typical AmeriSuites hotel offers its guest upscale amenities in an attractively designed suite with twenty-five percent more room space than a traditional hotel room. With demonstrated brand building and operational capabilities, Prime owns, manages, and has developed or franchised over 230 hotels throughout the nation. Prime currently ranks as the fifth largest hotel management

❖

Above: AmeriSuites Tulsa offers reliable service and comfort, and is staffed at every level with outstanding and dedicated employees.

Below: AmeriSuites Tulsa is located at 7037 South Zurich Avenue.

company in the nation, with a net worth of over $600 million and close to $1.2 billion in assets. Prime's success as a franchiser is based on years of experience as an operator and franchisee for hundreds of brand-affiliated and independent hotels.

Late 2004 brought a new owner into AmeriSuites corporate family. The Blackstone Group, originally founded in 1985, opened its first small office with a staff of four, including the two founders Peter G. Peterson and Stephen A. Schwarzman, a balance sheet of $400,000, and set of important core beliefs. They included the philosophy that, in a world of giant organizations with a broad array of services, there is room for a small firm with the highest levels of professionalism and strength, supporting strong management teams; in the 1980s world of hostile takeovers, the firm would only invest capital in strictly friendly situations, supporting strong management teams; in a world of ever larger firms, there are gifted, entrepreneurial professionals who, in a more personal setting, with institutional credibility and congruent goals, would join Blackstone in creating affiliated businesses in their area of expertise; in a world of "other people's money," the firm would always put significant amounts of its own money in investments it made, in a world rife with conflicts of interest, there was a need for a firm able to provide entirely objective advice and counsel without any pressure from alternative agendas. The Blackstone team's success in pursuing those goals and beliefs is reflected today in the firm's outstanding

reputation and its acknowledged role as a major global player.

With such diverse and well-positioned corporate bodies in place, AmeriSuites Tulsa continues as one of the premier destinations for travelers to the area. For reservations at AmeriSuites Tulsa, please visit www.amerisuites.com or call 918-491-4010 to speak with General Manager Bob Lowrance or any of his fine hotel staff for more detailed information.

❖

Top: Rooms at AmeriSuites Tulsa include a comfortable living area for guests.

Above: Guests of AmeriSuites know that home is not the only place to enjoy a comfortable bed and a good night's rest when visiting or working in Tulsa.

Left: Guests are particularly fond of the many amenities available at AmeriSuites, including a well-equipped fitness center.

LAFARGE TULSA CEMENT PLANT

A world-class operation dedicated to serving its customers, communities and employees, the Lafarge Tulsa Cement Plant continues a tradition of excellence that began nearly a half century ago. The plant's success was built on a consistent commitment to excellence, a safe working environment, and an active, positive relationship in and around the community. Since Lafarge's acquisition of the facility in 2001, these same principles of operating remain a priority.

The Tulsa Cement Plant, situated on 1,235 acres and set atop a limestone formation with more than forty years of remaining reserves, has been producing materials for the construction industry since 1961. It was the dream child of brothers Frank and Herbert Tyler, who founded the Dewey Portland Cement Company in Dewey, Oklahoma in 1907. The Tulsa site served as an ideal source for high quality raw materials. Its proximity to major markets, water transportation, and two turnpikes also ensured that 2609 North Fourteenth East Avenue was the perfect site. It's no wonder Dewey's Tulsa Cement plant opened to much fanfare in 1961.

Forty years later, Lafarge acquired the Tulsa Plant from the United Kingdom based Blue Circle Industries. Dewey had become a division of industrial products giant American-Marietta Company when its Tulsa plant opened in 1960. Blue Circle Industries, formerly known as Associated Portland Cement Manufacturers Ltd., began developing interests across the United States, in places such as the Tulsa plant, throughout the 1980s and 1990s and had become the sixth largest cement producer in the world. With its acquisition by Lafarge Corporation in July 2001, the Tulsa plant became part of the world's leading producer of cement and building materials.

In its first full year of operation by Lafarge, production capability topped 235,000 tons of cement—with only one kiln, one raw mill and one finish mill. Since that time, another kiln, raw mill, and two more finish mills have increased production capability to an astounding 850,000 tons per year. Customer pick-ups and deliveries occur at the plant, as well as at terminals located in Oklahoma City and Springfield, Missouri.

Creating the finest cement is an amazing process that begins in the quarry. Here, Lafarge employees extract limestone, which is crushed and transported by a conveyor system to mix silos. The raw materials, shale, sand, iron ore, and limestone, are then mixed together and heated to over twenty-six hundred degrees Fahrenheit in the kiln, becoming "clinker." When the clinker emerges from the kiln, it is cooled, mixed with gypsum and ground into a fine powder known as Portland Cement. This cement is then pumped into large storage silos for shipping and distribution. The bulk cement is then loaded onto trucks and railcars and shipped throughout the region or bagged for distribution.

This is a mammoth process that keeps kilns operating twenty-four hours a day, seven days a week resulting in 766,000 tons of cement produced in 2004 within a total grind capacity of 811,000 tons. Lafarge holds a cement

✧

Raw material is heated in cement kilns, shown here, to about twenty-six hundre degrees Fahrenheit to produce "clinker," which is then interground with gypsum to produce cement.

leadership position not only in the greater Tulsa metropolitan area but also across the State of Oklahoma.

High quality cements from the Tulsa Plant are used for a broad range of projects that include the I-40 emergency bridge replacement, the Tulsa's Creek and Cherokee Turnpikes, the new additions to both the St. Francis and St. John's medical complexes in Tulsa, the Oklahoma State University's Boone Pickens Stadium, the Northwest Arkansas Regional Airport, the Bud Walton Arena and the Razorback stadium addition in Fayetteville, Arkansas.

Backed by the strong partnerships Lafarge builds with its communities, Tulsa employees hail from all across Green Country, including Nowata, Sand Springs, Beggs, Wagoner and Skiatook. Characterized by their dedication and professionalism, Lafarge employees proudly participate in many company sponsored programs. They provide time, money and in-kind resources to agencies such as the public school systems in Collinsville and Catoosa, Junior Achievement, Up with Trees, Habitat for Humanity, and the Laura Dester Shelter for Children in Tulsa and various local charities and sports teams.

Lafarge's environmental leadership is legendary. By practicing a consistent commitment to preserving and protecting the environment, the company has made steady advances in environmental preservation and developed and successfully implemented numerous strategies and programs across North America. The Tulsa plant has invested millions of dollars in environmental controls and continuous improvement. It is committed to working with wildlife experts toward sustainable development in the area and serves as an active, positive force in the community, working toward cleaner and greener operations. The Tulsa plant recently implemented a plan establishing a nature habitat on a portion of its rehabilitated acreage and supports the Nature Conservancy, Wildlife Habitat Council and the World Wildlife Fund. Lafarge has a global partnership with World Wildlife Fund and Habitat for Humanity International.

For more company and product information visit the Lafarge North America website at www.lafargenorthamerica.com or call 918-437-3902.

Lafarge North America is the United States and Canada's largest diversified supplier of construction materials such as cement and cement-related products, ready-mixed concrete, gypsum wallboard, aggregates, asphalt and concrete products. The company's materials are used in residential, commercial, institutional and public works construction across the United States and Canada. In 2004, net sales exceeded $3.7

✧

Lafarge is committed to the principals of sustainable development. With the help of wildlife experts, the Tulsa plant has established wetlands habitats (one area shown here), which have been certified with the Wildlife Habitat Council.

CEDAR ROCK INN BED & BREAKFAST

The story of Cedar Rock Inn, a unique bed and breakfast in the rolling hills just west of Tulsa, is the story of a forgotten piece of Oklahoma history brought back to life by the artistic vision of Randy and Sandi Dittmann. The couple spent six years restoring the local landmark with roots in the last century and giving it new and relevant life for the new millennium.

The Dittmanns came to Tulsa from farming backgrounds. Randy grew up next to his grandfather's dairy farm in Buffalo, New York. He came to Oklahoma in 1980 and quickly became a dedicated Tulsan. A successful businessman, he established himself in the abstract and title business. He is a member of the American and Oklahoma Title Associations and has served as president of Tulsa Credit Association.

As a life long member of the Tulsa Rugby Club, Randy served many years as its president, captain and board member. He now volunteers for community youth rugby and has been Commissioner of the Green Country High School Rugby Council since its inception.

Sandi Dittmann was born and raised in the farming community of Miller, Missouri. She came to Tulsa in 1981, and after twenty years in banking, turned her attention to her love of art and her commitment to recycling and environmental awareness. As a respected local artist, the *Tulsa World* has featured her in the annual Philbrook Museum Festival of Trees. Sandi is an active member and past president of Tulsa Herb Society.

The Dittmanns' married in 1986 and their rural lifestyle led them to the hills just west of Tulsa where they discovered and renovated their current home in 1989.

In 1998 they bought the adjoining property that is now Cedar Rock Inn. At the time it was a neglected private residence built on land that was once allotted to the Creek Indian Nation in 1852 by the U.S. government. The first recorded owner was Tecumseh Perryman. Perryman was a prominent member of the Creek family that produced two tribal Chiefs and the first postmaster of Tulsa. In 1890, Perryman built a one-story house and later added a second story. With time, the house and the grounds fell into disrepair.

As they began the renovation, their vision grew and their plans for a modest historic home took on new significance. Along with master craftsman, Mark Laley, they designed a blueprint that would expand the structure into a showpiece, while preserving the integrity of the original dwelling.

Every inch of the house and grounds was painstakingly recreated. The interior was stripped down to the studs, while preserving some of the original trim, flooring and fixtures. A new addition was added that would include a large suite, kitchen, and dining room, complete with a forty-foot tower topped with oak beams and a copper lined cupola.

In keeping with their desire for authenticity, many of the features were made with materials native to Oklahoma. The doors and trim were hand built and milled locally from oaks, pecan and pine trees. The new dining room was crafted with a ceiling made of individual oak panels and a native flagstone floor.

In order to blend the new addition seamlessly into the house, Randy found, and moved, tons of the native sandstone that matched the exterior. New copper flashings and cedar shingles accentuate the beautiful stone.

Sandi spent countless hours scouting auctions, flea markets and incorporated authentic family period pieces to furnish the inn. She selected the very best of modern fixtures and technologies for the kitchen, seven bathrooms and a wireless Internet network.

Every effort was made to use recycled materials in the construction. The drive that leads to the front door was hand laid with 80,000 street pavers that were once a Coffeyville, Kansas street in the 1920s. The seven car carport, pottery and art studios were built with hundred-year old barn wood, much of which they had salvaged from an old barn in Nebraska.

Not only was the house completely renovated, the grounds also underwent a major transformation. Acres of lawn were designed, split rail fencing and a stone pillared gate was built. New limestone planters were filled with hundreds of azaleas and native plant beds developed. Even the pond on the front lawn was dredged and restructured to include a sparkling fountain and a waterfall.

The completion of many years of work and dedication is now seen in every aspect of the re-invigorated inn. Each of the bedrooms blends antique furnishings with the most luxurious linens. The private, glass tile baths each have their own special features such as saunas, whirlpool tubs and dual showers.

From their original intention of rescuing and refurbishing a piece of history, the Dittmanns' vision evolved into creating the work of art the house is today. By sparing no expense and allowing the craftsmen the gift of time, they have blended the preservation of the past with the very best the modern world has to offer.

The Dittmanns have brought their commitment to art, preservation of the past, and their deep ties to the community to every step of the process of bringing back a unique piece of Oklahoma history. From its earliest beginnings as a stagecoach stop, to its days as a mid-century private residence, to its final re-birth as a bed and breakfast, they believe that Cedar Rock Inn will thrive well into the twenty-first century as a new Tulsa landmark.

ONEOK, Inc.

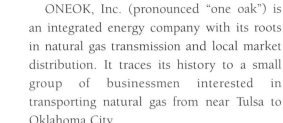

ONEOK, Inc. (pronounced "one oak") is an integrated energy company with its roots in natural gas transmission and local market distribution. It traces its history to a small group of businessmen interested in transporting natural gas from near Tulsa to Oklahoma City.

Dennis T. Flynn, a territorial congressman, and his partner, C.B. Ames, saw an opportunity. A small brick manufacturing plant in the Tulsa area was already using natural gas supplied from the natural gas discoveries in northeastern Oklahoma. But Oklahoma City and some surrounding towns were being served with manufactured gas. The businessmen reasoned that natural gas could be transported to the Oklahoma City area at a profit.

Joining Flynn and Ames in the project were two of Oklahoma's prominent pioneers in the petroleum industry, Glenn T. Braden and Theodore N. Barnsdall. Oklahoma Natural Gas Company was formed and articles of incorporation were filed at the Oklahoma Territorial Capital in Guthrie on October 12, 1906. It took a hundred miles of twelve-inch pipe to link Tulsa to Oklahoma City, with connections to serve Shawnee and Guthrie.

Nearly three quarters of a century later, on December 9, 1980, the company's overall activities had significantly evolved beyond the scope of its given name and shareholders agreed that the company's name be changed to ONEOK, Inc. The intent was that this new name would transform the historical perception of the

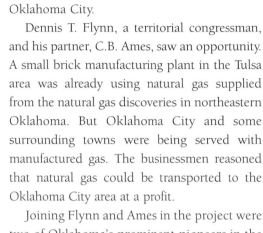

company and reflect a solid foundation in the utility business with increasing success and growth in non-utility areas. The distribution company continued serving its Oklahoma customers as Oklahoma Natural Gas Company.

ONEOK's long and successful experience in Oklahoma is characterized by a number of unique chapters in its rich history. During World War II, the coffee break emerged as a popular mid-day escape and most downtown Tulsa employees took their break at the Alvin Plaza Hotel, which was next door to the Oklahoma Natural Gas Company building. When the price of a cup of coffee went from a nickel to a dime (and only half cup refills were available because of the scarcity of coffee), company President Joseph Bowes exclaimed that he "didn't want his employees to have to pay a dime for coffee." A company break room on the mezzanine of the building was the result.

In the early 1930s, a young woman named Mildred R. Clark was hired to fill the newly created job of home service director to sell natural gas to homemakers. Many a customer remembers the Oklahoma Natural Gas home economists that provided recipes, cooking information and appliance tips to homemakers, Girl Scouts and home economics students. In fact, "gas company" nostalgia is so

❖

Above: Oklahoma Natural Gas Company building construction, circa 1928.

Below: Natural gas pipeline connection site.

strong that a book containing popular recipes and company history is now in its second printing. *Blue Flame Favorites* is available through Oklahoma Natural Gas Company.

The company was also an early pioneer in the use of television to reach consumers when, in 1949, the company aired the *Lookin' at Cookin'* television show on Tulsa's KOTV. The show, later called *Coffee Break*, was broadcast through 1980, making it the longest running single-sponsored television program of its time.

Though the utility would spend its first twenty years headquartered in Oklahoma City, in 1928 it moved the center of its operations to Tulsa and its newly completed Oklahoma Natural Gas Company building at 624 South Boston.

This was Tulsa's second building to be designed in the Art Deco tradition and it helped pave the way for the host of Art Deco buildings that followed. Currently listed on the *National Register of Historic Places*, the ten-story building was constructed of reinforced concrete, enclosed with buff, tapestry brick and trimmed with Indiana limestone and vitreous tile.

Ultimately, the company's enormous growth and industry success brought it to its current headquarters in downtown Tulsa. Eighteen-story ONEOK Plaza, at 100 West Fifth Street, was completed in 1984.

Today, ONEOK is a diversified energy company involved in natural gas production, gathering, storage, transmission and energy services. Additionally, successful processing facilities mean that ONEOK is one of the nation's top ten suppliers of natural gas liquids. Also, it is the general operating partner in one of the premier interstate pipeline partnerships in the U.S.

ONEOK is the largest natural gas distributor in Kansas and Oklahoma, and the third largest in Texas, operating as Kansas Gas Service Company, Oklahoma Natural Gas Company and Texas Gas Service Company, respectively. It provides natural gas service to more than two million retail customers in those three states, with 800,000 of those being in Oklahoma. And, through its energy services segment, ONEOK sells gas to wholesale customers and

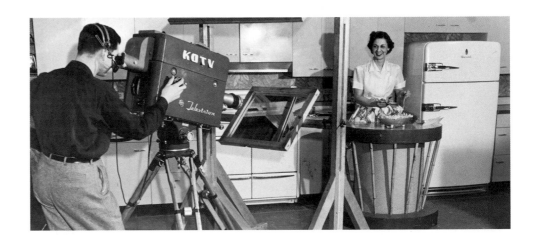

large-volume users in nearly every state in the union.

More than 4,600 dedicated employees ensure ONEOK's continued success as they prepare to celebrate the ONEOK centennial in 2006.

ONEOK offers safe, reliable energy and services to a diverse customer base. Following a strategy that blends the performance and profitability of all the segments, ONEOK has a balanced business mix that enables it to deliver sustainable earnings growth for the shareholders. Its vision is to be the premier energy company, developing assets along the energy chain to create exceptional value for all stakeholders.

ONEOK's leaders have always believed in giving back to the communities the company serves. Nowhere is this more evident than in its hometown.

In 2004, ONEOK received an award from the Tulsa Chapter of the Association for Women in Communications for its support of women in the worlplace and it was honored for business leadership by the Metropolitan Tulsa Urban League. It also received the 2004 Community Service Award from the Southern Gas Association.

For its long involvement with the arts, ONEOK received the corporate leadership award from the Oklahoma Arts Council in 2004. Additionally, ONEOK supports Philbrook Museum of Art, Gilcrease Museum, Oklahoma Jazz Hall of Fame, Tulsa Performing Arts Center Trust, Tulsa Ballet Theatre and the Tulsa Historical Society.

ONEOK is a Fortune 500 company listed on the New York Stock Exchange under the symbol OKE. On the Internet go to www.oneok.com.

Above: Oklahoma Natural Gas Company's Lookin at Cookin' *television program.*

Below: ONEOK's Tulsa headquarters today.

RODEWAY INN & SUITES

✧

Above: Rodeway's manicured lawns and modern amenities are a welcome site for travelers from across the country and around the world.

Below: Rodeway offers full executives suites with many of the amenities of home.

What started as an idea for a business venture shared between four friends over dinner one evening grew into what is now Rodeway Inn & Suites by Choice Hotels. Vice President of Franchise Sales for Candlewood Hotel Company, Charles "Chick" Armstrong, Senior Partner Lamb & Kawakami, LLP, Kevin Lamb, and President and CEO Packard Management Group Michael Goldstein, met with Jack de Boer, founder of Candlewood

Hotel Company and were immediately sold on the Cambridge Suites concept. DeBoer's ideas included the renovation and re-opening of Generation 1 Residence Inn by Marriott hotels into the Cambridge Suites product. The hotel was purchased after September 11th and renovation of the site that once housed a Residence Inn and Guesthouse International began shortly thereafter. The hotel operated successfully as Cambridge Suites by Candlewood for two years, until the dissolution of that brand gave way to the purchase of Rodeway Inn & Suites by Choice Hotels franchise in February 2004.

In January 2002, Nu-Gen Hotels LLC gained ownership of the property at 8181 East Forty-first Street and entered into a management contract with Packard Management Group of San Diego, California. Nu-Gen Hotels entered the twenty-first century with development plans for hotels across the United States, with peak interest in Tulsa, Oklahoma. The all-suite hotel has adopted a focus on the "extended stay" and corporate traveler with many of the same amenities one would find at home. Nu-Gen Hotels strives to exceed their customer's expectations by providing a great metropolitan atmosphere with spacious suites offering separate sleeping areas and fully equipped kitchens with standard size appliances. Spacious, executive size work desks, data ports, and compact disk alarm clocks are standard in every room.

Two unique "suite options" are offered by Rodeway Inn & Suites. The luxurious Executive Suite, averaging fifty percent more space than typical hotel rooms, includes a queen bed and bath, twenty-seven inch television with movies and VCR, hair dryer, iron and ironing board, breakfast bar, full-size refrigerator and range, voice mail, data port, two separate phone lines, a fireplace in some suites, and a large living area. The Penthouse Suite, averaging seventy-five percent more space than typical hotel rooms, provides guests with two spacious levels, two bedroom areas and two baths, a

sofa sleeper, twenty-seven inch television with movies and VCR, hair dryer, iron and ironing board, breakfast bar, full-size refrigerator and range, voice mail, data port, two separate phone lines, a fireplace, and a large living area.

A complimentary continental breakfast is provided daily along with a free *USA Today* newspaper Monday through Friday, while an outdoor pool and sports court, and on-site exercise room fully equipped with treadmills, exercise bikes, stepping machines and weights allows guests to maintain their fitness regimens while traveling. Free local phone calls, a free video and compact disk library, and a guest laundry facility as well as valet dry cleaning service are also available to guests. A business center with high speed Internet access in a separate room off the lobby enables guests to work twenty-four-hours a day.

Through franchise with Choice Hotels International, guests of Rodeway Inn & Suites can take advantage of the Ea$y Choice rewards program to earn points redeemable for free night stays or frequent flyer airline credit and the piece of mind associated with staying in hotels that franchise thousands of properties internationally.

Rodeway Inn & Suites is AAA approved and conveniently located in mid-town Tulsa, off the Broken Arrow Expressway or I-44 East at the Memorial Drive Exit, and is only six miles from Tulsa International Airport or downtown Tulsa, near a variety of restaurants, Woodland Hills shopping mall and the unique Brookside area as well as the enviable shopping sites and eateries of Utica Square, and a variety of entertainment venues.

Rodeway Inn & Suites proudly participates as sponsors to the Palmer Group Drug Abuse Programs, Oral Roberts University, and lends a hand to many private schools and organizations in the community through not only donations of services, but of their time.

To make a reservations or find out more information about Rodeway Inn & Suites please visit www.rodewaytulsa.com and www.packard-1.com, or by calling 918-664-7241.

✧

Top, left: A luxurious continental breakfast awaits Rodeway guests.

Above: Guests always appreciate the fully equipped, on-site fitness center available at Rodeway.

Below: This penthouse kitchen offers a home-away-from-home atmosphere as guests unwind from a long day of business or travel.

SAINT FRANCIS HEALTH SYSTEM

As a not-for-profit healthcare organization, Saint Francis Health System has been guided by a commitment to excellence, dignity, justice, integrity, and stewardship since opening in 1960. Extending the presence and healing ministry of Christ, this cutting-edge health system includes nearly 800 physicians and 6,600 employees collaborating with others who share its values to be the regional leader in the delivery of quality Catholic healthcare services.

Licensed for 918 beds, Saint Francis Hospital is widely known for its advanced technology and its excellent physicians. For several consecutive years, the hospital has been the recipient of National Research Corporation's Consumer Choice Award. Saint Francis has been named a Top 100 hospital by Solucient and listed among "America's Best Hospitals" by *U.S. News and World Report*.

Laureate Psychiatric Clinic and Hospital offers mental-health service to individuals and families and has an internationally recognized eating disorder program. Saint Ann's at Laureate Senior Diagnostic Center provides assessment and treatment of older adults needing mental heathcare.

The Children's Hospital at Saint Francis provides medical care to children in a child-friendly environment and includes 126 beds and a staff of 95 pediatricians and 45 pediatric sub-specialists. The hospital's pediatric hematology-oncology clinic, the only such facility in eastern Oklahoma, treats more than seven hundred children each year. In 2004, it became a member of The Children's Miracle Network, a nonprofit organization dedicated to helping children by raising funds for children's hospitals nationwide.

Early in 2005, Saint Francis Health System announced plans to construct a new 155,000-square-foot Children's Hospital, to be located on the northeast side of the hospital campus at Sixty-first and Yale. The project includes additional space for medical/surgical inpatient stays and a pediatric intensive care services. Child and family-friendly rooms will be coupled with parent education opportunities and a Child Life staff will help children become more at ease during their hospital stay.

Patients of the Natalie Warren Bryant Cancer Center have access to comprehensive cancer services, including a pediatric oncology/hematology clinic, blood and marrow transplantation program, specialized services provided by the inpatient adult medical oncology unit, and the most advanced radiation treatments, such as Intensity Modulated Radiation Therapy (IMRT). The Saint Francis Breast Center was relocated to the new Natalie Medical Building in early 2005, where diagnostic services were expanded to include breast MRI, genetic testing, bone densitometry and further support and assistance to breast cancer patients.

The Natalie Medical Building also houses the Saint Francis Surgery Center, which provides the most advanced minimally invasive surgical procedures available. It includes eight operating rooms equipped with voice activation, image management solutions and state-of-the-art surgical equipment. A post anesthesia recovery unit, eighteen rooms for outpatient admitting and discharge, six pain management assessment rooms and two pain management procedural suites with cutting-edge fluoroscopy equipment are also included at the Surgery Center.

The Saint Francis Imaging Center offers the latest in diagnostic radiology, Nuclear Medicine,

Magnetic Resonance Imaging (MRI), Computerized Axial Tomography (CT) Scan, and Ultrasound. The all-digital facility offers state-of-the-art technology in a customer-focused environment.

Warren Clinic, Saint Francis Health System's extensive network of primary and specialty physicians, provides easy access with locations scattered throughout Tulsa and surrounding communities (Broken Arrow; Coweta; Jenks; Owasso; Sand Springs; Stillwater; Tulsa; Bixby; Vinita; and McAlester.) A recent merger with Springer Clinic makes Warren Clinic the largest private medical group in the state.

Saint Francis Heart Hospital, the state's first freestanding, state-of-the-art specialty heart hospital, is the result of an innovative partnership between leading regional cardiovascular specialists and the Saint Francis Health System. It is the pinnacle of convenience and patient care and offers a wide range of services, including diagnostic testing, open-heart surgery, cardiac angiography, and medicated coronary stents. Dedicated to the prevention, diagnosis and treatment of cardiac and vascular disease, this fifty-two-bed facility was named by GE Medical Systems Information Technology as "one of the most advanced, all digital heart hospitals in the world."

To serve the needs of Tulsa's rapidly growing southern sector, Saint Francis Hospital at Broken Arrow has expanded its physicians' office and in-hospital acute care capacity. Diagnostic and outpatient services continue to expand as the needs of additional patient convenience grow.

Saint Francis Health System is evidence of the generous spirit of its founder, W. K. Warren, Sr. Along with his wife Natalie, W. K. supported numerous charities, but his dream was to build a hospital. He once told the *Tulsa World,* "We are anxious to build this hospital because the city has done so much for us."

Today, that dream is certainly a reality. Commenting on the development of new facilities such as The Children's Hospital at Saint Francis, President and Chief Executive Officer Jake Henry, Jr., wrote, "As northeastern Oklahoma's leading provider of pediatric services, the Saint Francis Health System too has been working toward the development and implementation of a master facility plan—one that would not only address and serve the needs of patients today, but establish a solid foundation for this organization to meet the needs of the community in the years ahead."

❖

Saint Francis Hospital.

VIKING PACKING SPECIALIST

Rex and Judy Graves, native Oklahomans from Leonard and Okmulgee, founded Viking Packing Specialist in June 1979. Rex was the vice president of a Tulsa Export Crating Company, which overextended in Houston, Texas and went broke. With $10,000 loaned from Judy's parents, the business was launched with no bank, no credit, a national truck strike, Jimmy Carter's twenty percent prime interest rates and an embargo on shipments to Russia. How did they make it? Rex has always said,"Fear is a helluva motivator!"

Building on local contacts, Viking began with orders from an ex-catcher with Dupont, an ex-second baseman from Byron Jackson Pump, and a golf buddy from Con-Rad, Etc., Viking was open seven days a week for seventy-eight days before taking Labor Day weekend off. Customers paid C.O.D., and with no credit, the company soon built a healthy checking account, and was offered credit terms. The need to perform at top levels was established during these times to justify the faith put in Viking by its friends and customers.

In early 1980, after just six months in business, Viking was approved for a $300,000 Tulsa Industrial Authority loan to purchase the land and building at our permanent headquarters at 10221 East Sixty-first Street, in Tulsa.

❖

Right: The Portable Medical Oxygen Unit was developed after the Valujet crash.

Below: Rex Graves stands with his plant manager of twenty years, Michelle Gillette.

Viking's early years primarily dealt with the oil related industries, i.e. heat exchangers, submersible pumps, refinery equipment, etc. The oil industry has gone through nine boom and bust periods in the company's twenty-five plus years. Survival has depended on the ability to get small quickly and to diversify as much as possible.

In the early 1980s, Viking began handling warehouse parts and shipments for Unit Rig and Equipment. Then the company went bankrupt in 1985, just as Centrilift, a Baker Hughes pump company sold a huge order to China. Within a span of two weeks, Viking went from bust to boom.

In the late 1980s, Viking began computer packaging for Telex. Texex had a tape drive, which was installed in big IBM mainframes. Viking's volume went from $900,000 per year to $2.3 million in 1988 and 1989. This was when Microsoft and Texas Instruments began making smaller and smaller computers. The

IBM project stopped abruptly in January 1990. Belt tightening time again!

Viking began looking at the new international laws governing the packaging of Hazardous Materials and ISO, the new International Quality Standards. Both ventures were costly and time consuming; however, the competition was not buying in.

Oil came back at this time and allowed the company the luxury of investing in these two areas. Bottom line, Viking is the only ISO Registered Packaging Company on the International Register. In our fields, Viking has no competition in Oklahoma for Hazardous Material Packaging, Testing and Haz-mat Schools.

In 1990, Viking began manufacturing ATA CAT I Spec 300 reusable containers for the Airline Industry. Viking has become the world leader in this field, as it is the only manufacturer who is qualified to test and certify these containers for hazardous materials.

Viking had reached $5 million in sales by 2001. The 9/11 disaster, "Rex's birthday" immediately threw the airlines into a tailspin. However, along came Lucent Technologies, referred to Viking by the Fed-Ex dangerous goods group in Memphis, Tennessee. Viking was the only qualified hazardous tester and packager for their 450# batteries for a communications plant in South Korea.

Eighteen months and $2 million later, it ended. Lucent was suddenly in financial shambles.

Enter the oil field again…. Baker Hughes Centrilift had grown steadily through the years and had solid contracts around the World at a time that oil began to rise to new record prices. Sales for Viking exceeded $5.2 million in 2004, its twenty-fifth year.

It's been a helluva ride, but these two Okies have weathered the storm. "Competition does not exist against Viking's

✧

Above: (From left to right) Virginia Bristol, Judy Graves, Drew Grant, Emma Broad and Michelle Gillette stand alongside a shipment of ATA Reusable Containers.

Below: Viking prepares to ship an Anhydrous Ammonia plant to Russia.

ORAL HEALTH PRODUCTS, INC.

Dr. Robert G. Jones and Beverly Stanton Jones started Oral Health in 1961. At the time, Dr. Jones was a successful practicing dentist in Tulsa.

Having started a young family and built a house, Doc and Miz B, as they were known, settled into the routine of a comfortable 1950s existence.

In his practice, Dr. Jones suffered along with his patients. Tooth decay and gum disease were the major focus of his efforts. At the time these two dental diseases were an enormous crisis for his patients.

Striving to give better service to his patients, and find the true cause of the problem, Dr. Jones came across the writings of Charles C. Bass, M.D., who was quietly researching the cause of these dental problems at Tulane University in New Orleans. Sitting at the feet of Dr. Bass, Dr. Jones learned that such diseases were preventable. The whole idea of preventive personal oral hygiene was a new and controversial idea. Simply by cleaning the teeth properly once a day, one could prevent a disease that had afflicted mankind for all time.

Drs. Jones and Bass became colleagues over time, and Doc would obtain from Dr. Bass the toothbrushes and dental floss necessary for properly cleaning teeth.

Toothbrushes and floss on the market at the time occasionally did more harm than good. The nylon of the bristles could harm gums and even enamel, because the tips of each little nylon bristle were sharp and rough. Dr. Bass determined that a soft nylon bristle, with care taken to polish the end so no sharp edges were left, would be the best type of bristle.

Graduate students earned credit for laboring in the basement of the Medical Arts building, gently polishing the tips of suitable toothbrushes, which would then be distributed to dentists trained in Dr. Bass' technique of personal oral hygiene. Dr. Jones went to talk with manufacturers of toothbrushes to see if they would make the type of bristles needed. None would, so Dr. Jones ended up at Dupont, who undertook the challenge as an engineering study.

Available dental floss was too thick. Dr Bass' specification for dental floss was "the thinner the better" was the way to go. Nylon extruded thin enough just could not be made with then current technology. Dr. Jones was part of a team that developed a method of extruding nylon to .0005" diameter.

Soon Dr. Jones' colleagues wanted this type of toothbrush and dental floss, but could not get the quantity necessary, so he started Oral Health Products, Inc. to produce them. The company literally began on the family's dining room table. Then moving to the garage, and on to Dr. Jones' dental office.

Doc and Miz B worked hard, raising a family, working at the dental office, and filling orders at night. After years of hard work, and demanding the highest quality, Oral Health grew into a company whose products are found worldwide.

P.O.H. brand dental floss went into space with the early astronauts as part of an experiment to see if the bacteria of the human mouth would change over time. The floss even went to the Moon with the Apollo missions.

Today, Oral Health Products, Inc. is certified to the international I.S.O. 9001-2000 certified quality management system standard. Doc and Miz B's family have seen to it that their legacy continues.

Oral Health Products, Inc. has continued to carefully manufacture soft, end rounded bristle brushes and the thinnest, finest dental floss to benefit patients.

Steering clear of faddish new trends in toothbrush design, their philosophy is that proper preventive personal oral hygiene is in your head, not in your hand. In keeping with that philosophy, efforts have

❖

P.O.H. toothbrushes are available in many styles and colors.

been made to improve the methods and processes that are used in manufacturing their products, with an eye to decreasing the cost to the consumer and improving the quality of workmanship.

P.O.H. (Personal Oral Hygiene) toothbrushes come in many styles and colors. In the production area, empty toothbrush handles whirl through automated equipment that fit them with bristles. A toothbrush is completed every two and a half seconds and kept in a sanitary environment. They retail at about a dollar, and still conform to Dr. Bass' original specifications.

P.O.H. floss comes in NoWax and LiteWax and is still unique. The dental floss is assembled carefully by knowledgeable technicians, proceeding through numerous quality imparting steps where modern

materials come together in the one of a kind cylindrical package known all over.

The newest item in the product line is Percept, a black dental floss designed to contrast with the plaque it removes from teeth. The company developed Percept so that dentists can teach and promote personal oral hygiene.

Current management credits the success of the company to its staff of nearly forty employees, who work hard everyday to make sure that P.O.H. toothbrushes and dental floss continue to help people around the world clean and keep their teeth.

In following with Doc and Miz B's desire to help share the gift of personal oral hygiene around the world, P.O.H. donates product to pro bono missions, shelters and schools where patients may not have access to professional oral healthcare. Dentists from all over take toothbrushes and floss to the farthest reaches of the globe. The company keeps pictures of "Smiley Kids" posted on their website. From Kansas City to Katmandu, P.O.H. is fulfilling the mission laid down by Doc and Miz B.

P.O.H. helps people clean and keep their teeth. For more information about P.O.H. products and the company's history, please visit www.oralhealthproducts.com.

✧

Above: Percept is the newest product for P.O.H. The black floss is designed to contrast with plaque it removes from the teeth.

Below: Dr. Robert and Beverly Jones.

QUIKTRIP

QuikTrip was conceived in 1958 over coffee and a chocolate shake.

Two former junior high school buddies–both, ironically, looking for exactly what the other had to offer–had high hopes that what later would be known as convenience stores could succeed in Tulsa.

The two friends, Burt Holmes and Chester Cadieux, were right. But success did not come overnight. Years later Cadieux would recall the countless mistakes that nearly killed QuikTrip in its infancy. "We learned everything by doing it wrong," he said.

Holmes brought the idea for the new business home after seeing 7-Eleven stores all across Dallas. He was convinced the concept of small grocery stores—some people called them bantam stores or drive-in groceries—could work in Tulsa.

But Holmes was not looking to operate the store himself. He needed a partner. He found one in Cadieux.

"I knew Chester to be bright and a hard worker…but I was very fortunate that he turned out to be nothing short of a management genius," Holmes would say later.

A native Tulsan, Cadieux was a graduate of the University of Oklahoma, had served in the

U.S. Air Force and was not afraid of a challenge. His work resume included selling peanuts at baseball games, washing mugs at Dairy Queen, picking peas one summer in Illinois, and earning the title as the top Fuller Brush salesman in Tulsa.

He was selling printing in 1958 but was not particularly enamored with that vocation. Cadieux possessed an entrepreneurial spirit. He dreamed of one day owning and operating his own business. Holmes' notion of introducing small grocery stores to Tulsa sounded like just the ticket.

Together with three friends, Holmes and Cadieux amassed $16,000 and incorporated the business on May 19, 1958. They called the business "Quik-Trip" because that is what they hoped their new business would be—an easy, quick trip for customers.

Four months later on September 25, 1958, the first QuikTrip opened on 5204 South Peoria in Tulsa. Unfortunately, jubilation over opening the company's first store did not last. Eight days after QuikTrip opened, the street in front of the store was temporarily closed. Sales were slow and could not entirely be blamed on the closed street.

✧

Above: Chester Cadieux at work in the 1960s.

Below: Chester Cadieux behind the counter at QuikTrip No. 1 in Tulsa.

"We didn't know the business," Cadieux says. "We stocked the wrong merchandise. We just didn't have the money to do it right."

Ironically, while Tulsa's newest entrepreneurs struggled to define their business, the customers who ventured inside No. 1 were not as clueless.

"They knew why they were there," Cadieux says. "They came on an impulse to buy something they wanted, just like our customers do today. They would ask for a single bottle of pop. Unfortunately, we didn't sell single bottles."

There was something else the customers liked about the first QuikTrip. They were drawn by the friendly young man behind the counter who always greeted them with a smile—and by name.

But a friendly smile and a penchant for learning his customers' names did not guarantee that Holmes and Cadieux's venture would go anywhere but under. A second store opened in February 1959. It was worse than the first. A third location started in July 1959. It immediately broke even and was soon profitable. By then all of the company's original $16,000 was gone, plus another $26,000 more.

Holmes remembers futile efforts at trying to raise additional capital for the struggling company.

"People would tell me years later what a great idea QuikTrip was," Burt says. "I remind them they didn't think it was such a great idea at the time."

But while bad locations and other mistakes were ravaging the company's finances, QuikTrip was quietly creeping toward success. A milk supplier agreed to finance a fourth store. It was an immediate success.

"Number four is the store that saved the company," Cadieux says.

Good locations and outside finance were not the only reason QuikTrip survived. Cadieux was both lucky and smart enough to invest in quality employees who helped turn his and Holmes' small venture into a world-class corporation.

QuikTrip is today often lauded for its ability to hire people with an energetic, entrepreneur spirit. Cadieux's ability to hire

these "quality" people did not come by accident. Hiring good people was a lesson Chester borrowed from the military.

"No matter what their rank, there were a few quality people you learned to count on to get things done," Chester said.

He remembered that lesson. From the earliest days of the company Cadieux made it a policy to hire only one person for every ten who applied.

"If you want to be the best, you have to be disciplined to hire the people you can count on," he says.

The company's earliest employees helped make April 30, 1962 among the most memorable in QuikTrip history. By then, seven stores were open and annual sales had topped $1 million. More importantly, the company had a net income of $21,370 and a stock book value of $1.04 per share.

"We had earnings, growth and history," Chester said. "We were a legitimate company. It was the happiest day of my life."

Today, Tulsa-based QuikTrip Corporation operates over 450 stores in nine states and boasts annual sales well over $5 billion. QuikTrip sells more than one percent of all the gasoline sold in the United States. The company ranks in the top forty on Forbes' list of Largest Private Companies. For the past several years QuikTrip been honored among Fortune's 100 "Best Companies To Work For."

❖

Today, QuikTrip has over 450 stores.

ZEBCO

Zero Hour Bomb Company seems a rather unlikely start for a business that today is one of the largest and best-known fishing tackle companies in the world—ZEBCO.

But it's true. It was time-detonated explosive devices used in the oilfields, not fishing products, being made at 1131 East Easton in Tulsa when opportunity came knocking in 1947.

At the door was R. D. Hull, a West Texas tinker who was looking for someone to build his concept for a new fishing reel "that won't backlash." Timing could not have been better because the Oklahoma business was facing expiring patents and changing technology of its products.

Company officials watched with interest as Hull used a Folger's coffee can lid mounted on a piece of plywood to show how a fixed spool design solved the tangled line problems, or backlashes, common to the revolving spool reels of the time. An idea, he explained, that came while watching a grocery store clerk pull string from a spool to wrap a package.

The rest, as they say, is history. The first twenty-five "Standards" came off the production line in June 1949. Five years later, the Model 33 was introduced. It wasn't long after that Zero Hour Bomb Company turned entirely to building fishing reels and shortened its name to ZEBCO.

The new ZEBCO push-button reels, (later dubbed "spincast" reels), made it easy for people of all ages and skill levels to enjoy fishing. In fact, to prove the point, one pioneering sales representative traveled sport shows with an identically dressed chimpanzee. After giving his sales pitch, he'd say, "It's so easy to cast, even a monkey can do it," and would hand the rod and reel to the chimp for a crowd-pleasing casting demonstration.

Sales boomed and ZEBCO needed more room. In the early 1960s, the company purchased land at 6101 East Apache Street and built its new headquarters there. ZEBCO still occupies the property today,

located near the Tulsa International Airport, and continues to expand and modernize the facilities. Just recently the company spent over one million dollars in building renovations. Another five million dollars has been invested in an on-site Research and Development center like the fishing tackle industry has never seen before. ZEBCO also has a two-hundred-thousand-square-foot shipping and distribution facility near Claremore.

In 2001, ZEBCO was acquired by the W. C. Bradley Company, a privately owned company headquartered in Columbus,

Georgia. Continuing to operate from its Tulsa hometown, the fishing tackle company has become an integral part of the W. C. Bradley Company.

Although the ZEBCO 33 is still a top seller (more than forty million have been sold) and closely resembles the original model of over fifty years ago, today's ZEBCO is much more than just a spincast reel company.

ZEBCO now manufactures and markets a full line of baitcast, spinning and fly fishing tackle—fresh and saltwater—under the top brand names of ZEBCO, Quantum, Rhino, Martin, Lew's, Van Staal and Fin-Nor. Among the product lineup are youth model ZEBCO rod and reel combos that sell for as little as ten dollars, all the way up to the finest of Fin-Nor precision engineered saltwater reels that retail for over $3,500.

From its earliest roots as Zero Hour Bomb Company to its present role as an industry fishing tackle giant, ZEBCO is proud to be Tulsa born and raised.

R. D. Hull originally showed his reel concept using a
Folger's coffee can lid on a piece of plywood

SPARTAN COLLEGE OF AERONAUTICS AND TECHNOLOGY

✦

Above: Spartan College of Aeronautics and Technology.

Below: Spartan's historic Aviation Hall.

Since 1928, Tulsa has been the proud home of Spartan College of Aeronautics and Technology—a one-of-a-kind, historic campus and aviation training center for men and women from across the country and around the world. More than eighty thousand technicians and pilots have graduated from the college and have offered their significant influence and extensive contributions to the aviation industry. Graduates are guided by a number of the most well-trained and outstanding teachers in receiving associate and bachelor degrees in programs such as professional pilot, aviation maintenance, aviation electronics (avionics), quality control, nondestructive testing, and communications. Working among the most influential names and companies in twenty-first century aviation, students have long taken pride in the Spartan name and its notable place in the history of Tulsa... and America.

That history began with the vision and confidence of W. G. Skelly, then president of Skelly Oil Company. Convinced that air transportation would eventually become commonplace, and thus require many skilled technicians and pilots, he established the Spartan School of Aeronautics and Spartan Aircraft Company on the grounds of the Tulsa Municipal Airport (now Tulsa International Airport) on September 27, 1928. Skelly's foresight met with great, and nearly immediate, success as enrollment in mechanic and flight

courses quickly established Spartan as Tulsa's "University of the Air" and the undisputed leader in aviation education.

As its reputation drew national, and then international attention, world famous oilman and wealthy entrepreneur J. Paul Getty acquired Spartan in the late 1930s. The tumultuous years of World War II and the Korean War lay ahead and Spartan's influence upon the field of civil aviation continued to expand. At the same time, thousands of its student pilots and mechanics began training for entry into America's armed forces.

Getty's formidable leadership during this period of Spartan history remains a landmark in its annals even today. In February 1942, Getty's daily guidance of the company and his great pride in America became characteristic of Spartan itself. By March, Spartan announced that seven NP-1 trainer planes had been delivered to the Navy in a single day. And in April the company officials proudly announced that all Spartan equipment, materials, and its entire company workforce had been donated to build another NP-1 trainer, christened the *Spirit of Spartan*. It was recorded by *The Spartan News* as possibly the first donation of its kind in aviation history.

The spring of 1943 brought the addition of another large three-hundred-thousand-square-foot section to Spartan's ever-expanding factory and allowed the company to become a major subcontractor to many of the nation's largest aircraft manufacturers.

Throughout the War, Spartan led the industry with outstanding quality and trustworthy efficiency. In 1961 a monument was erected to honor the efforts of Spartan during the war years. Dedicated to the memory of those trained at Spartan, it reads in part, "During World War II, sixteen thousand young men of the United States and Allied Nations received flight training at the Tulsa Municipal Airport and subsidiary fields. Of these, 14,000 were trained by Spartan School of Aeronautics and 2,000 by the United States Army."

As the aviation industry has continued to expand and grow around the world, so has Spartan. In 1944, Getty formed Spartan

Airlines, Inc., and was training TWA pilots in instrument flying techniques by 1945, and more than ten thousand G.I. Bill students would attend Spartan School by 1950. After Automation Industries, Inc., purchased Spartan in 1968, a multimillion-dollar campus was opened along Pine Street in 1969. In 1971, Spartan School of Aeronautics became a subsidiary of National Education Corporation (NEC), which ultimately became a subsidiary of Harcourt General Corporation in 1997. In 2001, Spartan Aviation Industries, Inc. formed and bought the Spartan School of Aeronautics, which became Spartan College of Aeronautics and Technology in 2004.

Yet it is the continuation of their diverse curriculum and innovative technological efforts that has held Spartan to its primary dedication to the higher education of aeronautics, the aviation industry and its related fields. With an average full time student population of 1,300 to 1,500 today, program costs and length vary depending upon a student's progress through the chosen course of study among three hundred thousand square feet of training facilities on three campuses and located at two of Tulsa's airports. Student housing is available at Spartan Landing and families are also assisted in locating local housing.

Spartan is accredited by the Accrediting Commission of Career Schools and Colleges of Technology and licensed by the Oklahoma Board of Private Vocational Schools. Most courses are approved by the Oklahoma State Accrediting Agency for Veterans, and the Federal Aviation Administration approves the aviation maintenance programs and flight programs.

The most effective, modern tools of aviation education are available to students of the college, and Spartan maintains industry-current equipment for hands-on training that prepares students for entry-level career positions. Four flight simulators and over fifty aircraft are maintained for flight training at Spartan, while continued placement services are always available to graduates.

In 2005, Spartan's president and chief executive officer, Terrell "Terry" W. Harrison, is honored to lead Spartan students into this "second century of the aviation industry." From Spartan's ability to provide practical, hands-on training to ensuring the highest quality career-oriented education programs and development strategies, this is the historic place "to train for a future in aviation...[and the] beginning of an exciting and rewarding new adventure."

College tours are available Monday through Friday from 9 a.m. to 4 p.m. and can be scheduled through the main campus admissions office by calling 800-331-1204, or visit Spartan's website at www.spartan.edu.

❖

The Radio Classroom at Spartan.

Moody's Jewelry, Inc.

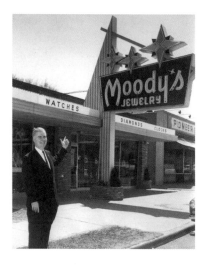

✧

Above: Ernest Moody, Jr. at his twelfth and Harvard location.

Below: Moody's at Utica Square.

Ernest Luther Moody, Jr., was born in Little Rock, Arkansas on May 7, 1925 to Ernest and Vashti Moody. A year later, the young family moved to Pitcher, Oklahoma, where Ernest, Sr. joined Vashti's father in building one of the first automatic steam-driven laundry facilities in the state. It was believed that family members were spreading tuberculosis as they washed their laundry together, so this new laundering process of sterilizing clothes would hopefully prevent the germ from spreading.

As the family ventured into the new business, Ernest, Jr. followed his mother throughout the neighborhood picking up and delivering loads of laundry. Ironically, mother and son would both be diagnosed with tuberculosis only a few years later. Though everyone in the family joined in the laborious work, the small town of Pitcher was hit dramatically in 1928 as the Great Depression settled across the country. Within a year, the fledgling laundry business closed and the family moved into Vashti's parent's home in Tulsa.

Amidst a difficult economy and health concerns at home, the summer of 1931 marked the humble debut of Ernest Jr.'s lifelong career in sales. His grandparent's home sat near a farmers market where Ernest would take fifty cents and his homemade wooden wagon to buy a bushel of corn. He then walked door-to-door selling three ears of corn for ten cents—he was only six years old!

This entrepreneurial spirit served Ernest well throughout his childhood and by the time he was thirteen he had built a wooden stand in his front yard where customers could buy everything from candy to soda pop to fireworks. He quickly learned that if he bought in quantity, priced fairly and worked hard, he could find a way to earn extra income to help his family and still have a little left over for him.

After his father's sudden death in 1939, Ernest saved every penny to take care of his mother. When the family alarm clock broke, he took it to J. R. Cupples, the owner of Gilmore's Repair Shop at 808 North Lewis. But with an estimated repair totaling $1, Ernest knew he could not pay the bill. The sympathetic repairman offered a solution–he would teach Ernest how to replace the broken spring, thus saving fifty cents for labor. When Ernest told him that he still didn't have the other fifty cents to buy the spring, Cupples offered him an after-school job to repay the debt. With that, the alarm clock was soon repaired and a seed was planted deep inside Ernest Moody, Jr.–a seed that would sprout and grow into a lifetime love affair with watches and jewelry.

In 1942, at the age of sixteen, Ernest again had to leave high school when a lung infection, tuberculosis, forced him to spend the next eighteen months in a sanatorium. As fate would have it, one of his roommates was an elderly watchmaker and the two were soon making repairs for patients, the staff and their families. It was there that Ernest arranged to print his first business card proclaiming Moody's Time Service.

Following his recovery, Ernest returned home to graduate from high school with honors. Though he received a scholarship to attend Cornell University to study electrical engineering, Ernest's mother was not doing well and it was difficult for him to think of moving away from her.

Once again, the paths of Ernest and Cupples were to cross and set in store his destiny. Cupples was ready to retire and he knew that Ernest showed a natural talent and appreciation for watch repair. When he decided to sell his business, he asked Ernest how much he could afford to pay. Ernest told him that he and his mother had saved just a little over $160 and that was all he had. Cupples decided on the spot that that was the exact value of his business and sold it to Ernest.

It was November 1944 and Ernest Jr., at the age of nineteen was now a business owner. He often worked sixteen hour a days, six days a week and did not have a lot–only a repair bench, some mostly worn out tools and a

box of watch and clock parts that were nearly two decades old. What he did have however, was a strong work ethic and a relentless, entrepreneurial spirit that would serve the business well into the twenty-first century.

With the business firmly established and a solid reputation in the neighborhood, things progressed nicely in Ernest's young career. He was also dating his future wife, Mildred LoRayne Nichols, a beautiful cashier at Getman Drugstore whom he had met at a church function.

It was 1946 and everything was coming together nicely when Ernest's landlord decided to more than double the rent on his space. Ernest took it as a sign that it was time to move and relocated the business to a developing suburban area east of downtown Tulsa near Twelfth and Harvard Avenue.

But it was not long after the move that Ernest developed life-threatening complications from his former lung condition. He handed over the shop keys and checkbook to Mildred and was taken to a military hospital in Denver for a new experimental surgery. Ernest was one of only several patients to recover with a long-term survival rate. In the meantime, Mildred and an eighty-year old retired watchmaker kept the customers happy until Ernest's return.

Ernest and Mildred have since raised five children, all of whom have joined the family business. Ernest III became its president and CEO in 1989. Emily Moody Boyd, Melinda Moody Claiborne, and Patricia Moody Kaltenbach all work at the company, and Kevin Moody serves as the company's vice president.

Today, Moody's employs over eighty full time employees serving a customer base that stretches across Northeastern Oklahoma and ranges in ages from 15 to 75. Present locations include Twelfth and Harvard Avenue, Fifty-first and Harvard Avenue, Fifty-first and Sheridan, Sixty-eighth and Memorial, Seventy-first and 145 East Avenue, Twenty-first and Utica, Seventy-first and Highway 169, and on the web at www.moodysjewlry.com.

Moody's Jewelry Inc. participates in many charitable and community organizations including Tulsa Boys Home, Habitat for Humanity, John 3:16 Rescue Mission, Big Brothers and Big Sisters, St. John's Hospital Foundation, Youth Services of Tulsa, Tulsa Area United Way, Rotary and Kiwanis Clubs, Young President's Organization, YWCA, Miss Oklahoma Pageant, Tulsa Executive Club, Executive Women International as well as numerous local public and private schools including the University of Tulsa, Oral Roberts University, Jenks, Tulsa and Union Public Schools.

Moody's continues to grow and expand as we study the market and economy in the Tulsa area. We are fortunate to have a loyal following of customers who regard Moody's as a long time, reputable family business who provide great service and unprecedented products to fit any need.

✧

Young Ernest Moody, Jr., at his original store.

SAND SPRINGS SCHOOL SYSTEM

Nestled along the Arkansas River and about eight miles from downtown Tulsa, the community of Sand Springs blends small-town charm with modern-day conveniences and offers citizens one of the oldest and most respected school districts in Tulsa County. It's the type of place where former students return as teachers and retired teachers become hometown heroes and the school carnival is still the hottest ticket in town. With a challenging curriculum, outstanding special education programs, and the most comprehensive vocational instruction in the

state, Sand Springs Public Schools has built a reputation as a district worthy of its motto, "Setting the Pace with Quality Teaching."

In close partnership with the community, Sand Springs Public Schools strives to create a safe, positive environment to empower, enable, and inspire lifelong learners through quality education. All school district employees have the highest quality of professional growth and development opportunities, however, Sand Springs Public Schools encourages success in every student and ensures all will reach their full potential as respectful and responsible citizens.

Students of the Sand Springs Public School District not only perform well in state-mandated testing programs year after year, but the graduating class of 2004 earned scholarships totaling $397,230 for one year and $1,350,734 for four years, and featured fifty-five Honor Graduates and twenty-four Oklahoma Academic Scholars.

The future of Sand Springs Public Schools is very bright indeed. In 2003-2004, during the state's economic difficulties, the Sand Springs Education Foundation spearheaded a fund-raising effort, Operation Gold Pride, that exceeded its goal and raised $640,000 to support the implementation of full-day kindergarten and expand the early childhood opportunities in the district. As a result of this highly successful fund-raising campaign, the Sand Springs Education Foundation received the Excellence Award from the Oklahoma Foundation for Excellence in May 2004.

The community's positive connection to the school is also evident by the active Partners for Progress and strong voter turnout at polls when bond issues are being considered. The Partners for Progress, a committee consisting of school and community leaders, developed a twenty-year facilities improvement plan that the community supported with over eighty percent approval votes on recent bond elections. Parent organizations are actively involved in classrooms across the district and offer support to parents, students, and teachers throughout the school year.

ENARDO

Enardo has a rich history that was built in the oil fields of the United States and Canada. The company was founded by Phil B. Drane in 1933 and headquartered in Tulsa. The name of the company came about by taking Drane and spelling it backwards and adding an "O" to make Enardo.

The company was established as a leader in vapor control systems for oil field storage tanks. The combination of products became a system that prevented loss of product through evaporation and reducing corrosion. The early benefits were economic, but much later became supportive of environmental regulations related to clean air standards. The company grew to become the Enardo Foundry and Manufacturing Company in the 1940s and '50s.

Thanks to the ingenuity of Robert S. Tomer, Enardo is a company that literally came out of hiding after ten years. Tomer was working for a parent company named Centerline in the 1960s when he found remnants of the Enardo products. Tomer convinced a banker to loan him the money to purchase the products and started RST Service Manufacturing, which produced Enardo products. This move was the rebirth of the company that was eventually renamed Enardo.

Enardo now manufactures low pressure safety and environmental vapor control products that consist of pressure vacuum valves, flame arrestors and storage tank vents for the oil and gas, petrochemical, pharmaceutical, chemical, pulp and paper, and waste industries that assist in protecting people, property, and the environment. The company actively sells in thirty countries with three regional offices and over seventy representative sales offices.

Enardo is headquartered in Tulsa with its sales, manufacturing, engineering and administration located at the 32,500-square-foot plant at 4470 South Seventieth East

Avenue. The company also has a second site in Tulsa for its research and development laboratory, which is 6,850 square feet with adjoining acreage.

In 2004, Enardo maintains an employee base of approximately fifty people and revenues near $10 million annually. The customer base is worldwide and consists of all major and independent oil and gas companies, petrochemical companies, loading terminal operators, chemical companies, and pharmaceutical companies and many municipalities.

The company has grown under the Tomer family's leadership. Patric A. Tomer began his service as president in 1979 until the current president, Mark J. Tomer, took over in 1985. Under Mark's leadership, the company sales have grown at an average rate of 15 percent per year over the past 19 years. Enardo has an aggressive strategic growth plan over the next 5 to 10 years of tripling its size through market and territorial expansion, new product development and acquisitions, and operational efficiencies worldwide.

Enardo gives back to its community by donating to many charitable organizations in Tulsa, as well as supporting the Red Cross as a continual blood drive donor and United Way with employee matching funding, which recognizes the company with a Gold Award standing.

Business involvements include the Oklahoma Alliance for Manufacturing Excellence, Oklahoma Safety Council, Tulsa Area Manufacturers Association, and American Production and Inventory Control Society, National Association of Manufacturers, American Petroleum Institute, National Fire Protection Association, and the American Institute of Chemical Engineers, Business and Marketing Associates of Tulsa, the Oklahoma Society of CPAs and American Institute of CPAs.

✧

Top, left: Enardo Company employees in August 2004.

Above: Robert S. Tomer reestablished Enardo.

Below: Mark Tomer has served as the company's C.E.O. since 1985.

Carrera Gas Companies, L.L.C. is a natural gas gathering, processing and treating company founded in 1995. Since 1995, Carrera has acquired and assumed operations of several natural gas gathering and processing assets in Oklahoma and Texas.

Carrera owns at least fifty percent interests in four gas-processing plants and related gathering systems. Processing capacity of plants operated by Carrera is 108 million cubic feet per day and related pipelines total approximately 350 miles. Carrera operates those facilities as well as a facility for a third party.

Currently employing twenty-five people, Carrera is purposely structured for quick, responsive action. The structure enables Carrera to handle tasks with greater efficiency than larger companies.

Carrera consults with numerous oil and gas producers and investors regarding gathering, processing and treating facilities and actively seeks to purchase or build additional gathering and processing assets.

Robert W. Jackson and Robert W. Mitchell, III founded Carrera. Jackson is CEO and owns a majority interest in the company. Jackson began his gas-processing career with Cities Service Oil Company, where he was employed for fifteen years in the Natural Gas Liquids Division. In 1982 he founded Cimarron Gas Companies, L.L.C. In 1983 he was one of four founders of American Central Gas Companies, Inc.

Currently, Jackson serves as a director of the Gas Processors Association (GPA), having served on various committees and as an officer of GPA. Jackson served three years on the Propane Education and Research Council (PERC), including one year as vice chairman. He also served as a director of the Oklahoma Natural Gas Association.

Robert W. Mitchell, III owns the remaining equity in the company. In 1981, after obtaining a degree in Chemical Engineering from the University of Texas, Mitchell was employed by Perry Gas Company where he held positions in operations, design engineering, gas supply and business development. In 1986 he joined Rockland Pipeline Company and held management positions in operations and business development.

In 1991, Mitchell accepted the position of Manager of Operations with Cimarron Gas Companies, L.L.C., and joined Carrera in 1996.

❖

Above: Today, Carerra operates natural gas gathering and processing plants throughout Oklahoma and Texas.

Below: Bob Jackson and Robert Mitchell, III founded Carrera in 1995.

HOLLINGER & ASSOCIATES, INC.

Sam and Norma Hollinger, married in 1961, have enjoyed the business of homebuilding for nearly their entire life together. With Sam's love of architecture and Norma's affection for interior design, Sam began selling new homes in 1963 and founded Equitable Homes, Inc. in 1972. When their children began graduating from college in 1989, Sam wanted to create a company to involve them and Hollinger & Associates, Inc. was born.

The distinctive designs and unparalleled, Old World craftsmanship that have become a trademark of the company actually began with Sam's deep admiration for his grandfather, one of Tulsa's historic personalities, William G. "Billy" Bruner. A Lutcapoga Creek Indian and Chief of the Creek Nation, Bruner was born after his parents arrived in the area on the "Trail of Tears." He lived his entire life on his allotment in the Bruner Stations areas, which were named after him, on the Sand Springs line. Sam, mesmerized by his grandfather's now-famous stories of pre-statehood days in Oklahoma, was taught to appreciate the beauty of nature that could be found in and around Tulsa

His love for Tulsa and its honorable history served Sam well during his early years as a salesman, carefully watching the homebuilders and learning everything he could about the inner workings of the business. Later, his four children began working on the houses, doing sweep-outs and framing. When they became adults, Kimberlea became the company's property manager and salesman before raising three children of her own; Greg graduated from OU Architectural School and joined their company in Atlanta before moving back to Tulsa as a

designer and builder; Rob attended OSU and OU and became a builder in Atlanta; and Randy graduated from OU as a salesman for an international firm while his wife, Anna, is heavily involved in marketing and selling real estate.

Through the years, the firm has grown in size and stature. What once was a two-man operation now takes six people and over 250 subcontractors with the average price of the high-end custom and speculative homes ranging from $19,000 to $25,000 in 1989 to $450,000 to over several million-dollar homes today. Their homes have been featured in local, national and international magazines while their multi-million dollar *Porto di Cielo* was featured in the 2003 "Tulsa Street of Dreams." Such impressive growth is squarely measured by the firm's continued family tradition of service and quality to every client.

Charitable involvement plays a vital role in the company's commitment to serving their community. Both the fifteen-thousand-square-foot Domestic Violence Intervention Shelter and Youth Shelter of Creek County were not only built by Hollinger & Associates, Inc. but also funded by the donations they secured. The company also works with Habitat for Humanity, First United Methodist Church, Junior Diabetes, and the Brush Creek Youth Ranch Teen Challenge.

For more information about Hollinger & Associates, Inc., please call (918) 296-3433 or visit www.hollingerassociates.com.

✧

Above: Sam Hollinger lived with his grandfather in this small concrete block home. Pictured here are Sam, his grandfather, and Joe Bruner.

Below: Sam Hollinger's grandfather, "Billy" Bruner, was one of Oklahoma's living legends at the age of 106.

SULZER CHEMTECH USA

Sulzer Chemtech USA, as Nutter Engineering, traces its roots back to 1945, when Earl Nutter began investigating tray performance at the Panoma Corporation's Cargray Plant in White Deer, Texas. His goal was to develop a tray with better efficiency than the current technology of bubble-cap trays. His work led to the development of the rectangular valve tray, which revolutionized the industry. In 1951, the first Nutter valve tray was installed in a six-foot diameter absorber at a natural gas plant in Carson County, Texas. Following further development, Earl received a patent for his valve tray in 1955. That year, a Dallas firm acquired the Panoma Corporation and Earl set out on his own.

Hoping to license his invention, Earl built a portable distillation simulator in his garage to demonstrate the operation of his tray. He met with representatives from the major equipment suppliers, but none were interested in his valve tray. Determined to make it work, Earl moved to Tulsa and established Nutter Engineering in 1956. In 1961, Earl moved his business into a small office and fabrication facility at Sulzer's current location in West Tulsa.

Earl joined Fractionation Research Inc. (FRI) in 1962 and arranged a performance test of the valve tray. Unfortunately, the test results were poor and business began to fall off. Facing bankruptcy, Nutter Engineering was sold to Air-X-Changers in 1963. Earl stayed, and with the help of his son Dale, redesigned the valve tray. In 1964, FRI tested the "Type B" valve tray and the results were excellent. This was a turning point for the company. Sales increased and the company began to grow.

Earl continued at Nutter until 1969, when his health began to fail due to lung cancer. Following his father's death in 1971, Dale assumed his father's role and continued developing new products for Nutter Engineering. Dale received over forty patents during his career. In 1976, Air-X-Changers and Nutter Engineering were acquired by the Patterson-Kelley division of Harsco. This provided the financial backing required for continued growth of the company.

The company expanded its product line to include random and structured packings following development of the Nutter Ring and acquisition of Chem-Pro in 1984. During the late 1980s and early 1990s, the company operated a second sales office in Birmingham, England and cooperated with the Cana-Tex corporation to offer equipment installation and field services for the product line.

In 1998, Nutter was acquired by the Sulzer Corporation of Winterthur Switzerland, making Sulzer Chemtech USA, Inc. the second largest mass-transfer company in the United States. Sulzer Chemtech (www.sulzerchemtech.com) is active in the field of process engineering and employs some twelve hundred people worldwide. Sulzer Chemtech is represented in all important industrial countries and sets standards in the field of mass transfer with its advanced technical and economical solutions. The full product and service offering includes:

- Process components such as trays, structured and random packings, internals for separation columns and reaction technology;
- Engineering services for separation and reaction technology such as optimizing energy consumption, plant optimization studies, pre-engineering for governmental approval and basic engineering;
- Separation and purification of organic chemicals by means of crystallization and membranes; and
- Mixing and reaction technology with static mixers.

In 2000, Sulzer Chemtech USA began operating the Turnaround and Field Services division. This unit, based in Pasadena, Texas, provides installation and repair service throughout North and South America. In 2003, Sulzer acquired the mixing related business of Koch-Glitsch, making Sulzer's Mixing & Reaction Technology business the world leader and in a class of its own.

Today, the combination of the early Nutter developments and the "state of the art" technology developed at Sulzer makes Sulzer Chemtech USA a market leader in mass transfer and mixing & reaction technology, design, manufacture and installation.

✧

An early portable simulator.

In 1960, Al and Jenell Storey began to build their worldwide wrecker service empire with a small, two-pump, one-bay service station at Sixty-third Street North and Peoria Avenue. While Al worked at the MidContinent Refinery to pay the bills, Jenell kept things running smoothly at the station.

A few years later, the Storeys moved to a larger DX station at 4604 North Peoria Avenue. Much to the dismay of his wife, Al took out a second mortgage on their home to purchase his first wrecker from salvage—he named it "Little Red." As the business began showing a profit, they added more wreckers and Al retired from the refinery. Jenell remembered the period well, "It really got to be quite a job. We were towing for dealers and we also did a lot for the highway patrol."

In the early 1970's the Storeys moved to another service station at 742 North Lewis Avenue. Vehicles were stored on one of two lots, located on East King and Heavy Trafficway. By this time they had six or eight wreckers and decided to bid on the city contract, but were unsuccessful in their first attempt.

As the wrecker service continued to thrive, the Storeys decided to close their service station business and focus everything upon the wrecker business. Then, in 1973, they won the city contract for Tulsa and have maintained it, except for a short period in the mid-1980s, since that time.

Today the Storeys operate thirty-three wreckers and two service trucks, making their company the largest service of its kind in Oklahoma, and is located at Ten North Elwood Avenue in Tulsa and 775 North Redbud in Broken Arrow.

With the growth of their business, the Storey family has enjoyed giving back to their community in meaningful ways, and the unswerving generosity of their father Al has been their greatest example. From offering a hot meal and a $100 bill to a weary, down-on-his-luck patron at the Beacons Café, to giving his boots to a surprised service attendant and then walking out in his sock-feet, the stories of his life and example are legendary. Jenell helped curb drunken driving statistics through her innovative program, "Storey on Safety," providing free tows for people who

have had too much to drink and this was just one of her many passions for helping people.

Though the family lost Al in 1998 and Jenell in 1999, children Lisa, Brad and his wife Dana continue the company's tradition of excellence and are involved in the American Cancer Society and M.A.D.D., and provide pencils to students that are imprinted with the statement, "Don't Drink and Drive."

With over sixty well-qualified and invaluable employees today, Storey Wrecker Service, Inc. has set the standard for quality and service all across the continental United States and Canada by backing their distinctive service with experience, state-of-the-art equipment and skilled tow-men.

For more information about this historic Tulsa business, visit www.storeywrecker.com.

❖

Above: Al Storey.

Below. In 1987, the Storey family, Lisa, Brad and his wife Dana, and Al's wife Jenell, were featured on the cover of the Tulsa World's a local Oklahoma magazine.

ROMAN CATHOLIC DIOCESE OF TULSA

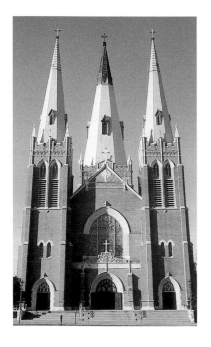

✧

Above: Holy Family Cathedral at Eighth and Boulder in downtown Tulsa.

Below: Most Reverend Edward J. Slattery, third bishop of Tulsa.

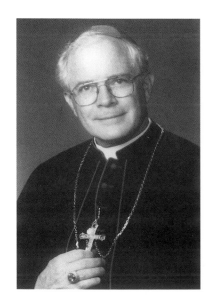

History records a Catholic presence in what is now eastern Oklahoma in 1541, when eleven missionary priests accompanied the DeSoto Expedition some twenty miles along the Arkansas River west of present-day Fort Smith. The 1800s again saw Catholic missionaries entering the region, and in 1872 the first Catholic church in the Indian Territory was built at Atoka, then the railhead of the Katy Railroad. The first Catholic bishop, the Belgian missionary Theophile Meerschaert, came to the Territory in 1891; his headquarters were at Guthrie, and he was responsible for what today is the entire state. It was not until 1973 that a separate Tulsa diocese came into being.

As early as the 1920s, Bishop Francis Clement Kelley, Oklahoma's second bishop, considered moving his cathedral and chancery from Oklahoma City to Tulsa. The Depression and other factors, however, frustrated that plan. Bishop Kelley was a strong leader who was open to many of the reforms of the Second Vatican Council years before these became the general trend of the Church worldwide. Kelley died in 1948 and Bishop Eugene J. McGuinness, who had served as coadjutor since 1945, became his successor.

Whereas Kelley's main interest had been in making converts to the Catholic faith, McGuinness was primarily concerned with providing priests to minister to them. During his thirteen years in Oklahoma, McGuinness dedicated 102 new church buildings, 70 rectories, 48 schools, 38 convents, 12 parish halls, 6 new hospitals, and 4 hospital additions.

Feeling the weight of his heavy schedule, McGuinness petitioned the Pope for an auxiliary bishop; and on December 5, 1957, Monsignor Victor Reed, rector of Holy Family Co-Cathedral in Tulsa, was appointed auxiliary to Bishop McGuinness. After McGuinness died of a heart attack later that same month, Reed was chosen to succeed him.

Plans for the Vatican Council were announced within a year of Reed's becoming a bishop and its reforms provided the guiding principles for much of his episcopate. The early experiments he permitted were well received by many, but they also brought angry complaints from others who felt their cherished traditions were being destroyed. Between 1964 and 1975 nearly one hundred diocesan and religious clerics left the priesthood.

In 1970 the bishop and his consultors began a study of the problems connected with the long-awaited division of the diocese. While this was going on, the priests of the Tulsa deanery met independently in March 1971 and voted to request the division. Before much else could be accomplished, however, Bishop Reed died suddenly in September. His successor was Bishop John R. Quinn, who was installed in January 1972.

Quinn cooperated with the process begun by Bishop Reed, and on December 17, 1972, it was announced that thirty-one counties in eastern Oklahoma had been set-aside as a new diocese, with Tulsa as its cathedral city. The diocese was formally erected on February 7, 1973, and Bernard Ganter, until then chancellor of the Galveston-Houston diocese, was ordained as the first bishop. Ganter was succeeded by Bishop Eusebius Beltran (1978-1992), who subsequently was promoted to the post of archbishop of Oklahoma City. Bishop Edward J. Slattery (1994-present) followed Bishop Beltran upon his promotion.

The Diocese of Tulsa, with its seventy-eight parishes, has continued to serve the eastern Oklahoma community in a number of ways, one of which is Catholic Charities of Tulsa, now under the direction of Timothy Sullivan. Catholic Charities has an extensive range of programs, including St. Elizabeth Lodge, which provides apartments for homeless families; Madonna House, for women with problem pregnancies; St. Joseph Residence, for patients and their families affected by AIDS; and services directed toward Asian and Hispanic newcomers to the United States.

Another important function of the diocese is the operation of schools, most notably Bishop Kelley High School, and a number of parochial schools in Tulsa and other cities. Other Catholic schools, such as Cascia Hall and Monte Cassino, along with institutions like St. John Medical Center and St. Francis Hospital, are owned and operated by independent religious orders and lay foundations, even though these share in the same Christian mission as the diocese.

The full story of the Roman Catholic Church in eastern Oklahoma is contained in *This Far by Faith: 125 Years of Catholic Life in Oklahoma, 1875-2000*, available from the Diocese of Tulsa, P.O. Box 690240, Tulsa, Oklahoma 74169-0240.

Charles Faudree's nearly four decades as an interior designer have allowed him to work throughout the United States and Europe. His designs have appeared in numerous publications including *Veranda, House Beautiful, Southern Living, Southern Accents, Traditional Home, Renovations Style,* and *House and Garden and Country Living.* Additionally, his work is displayed in a variety of decorating books such as *Garden Style, Country Living, Country Kitchens, Creative Ideas for Decorating, Decorating by Southern Living, Southern Accents Christmas, House Beautiful Christmas* and *Provencal and Holiday Homes.* Charles is also featured as one of eight designers in the book *Traditional Homes Signature Style.* He accepted the award for Traditional Home's Designer of the Year in 1995 and was chosen as one of the "Top Designers in America" by *House Beautiful* in 2002, 2003 and 2004.

Charles' first book, *Charles Faudree's French Country Signature,* was released by Gibbs-Smith Publishers to wide acclaim in 2003 and is now in its ninth printing with over fifty thousand copies sold. While he has promoted the book in lectures around the country, *USA Today* has joined many shelter magazines in writing feature articles on the work, as well. A second book,

Charles Faudree's Country French Living, was released in 2005.

Founded in 1970, Charles' interior design studio and retail shop are located at 1345 East Fifteenth Street in Tulsa, and on the web at www.charlesfaudree.com. Much like Charles' signature rooms, the Charles Faudree store features an eclectic mix of the casual and the formal, the old and the new. Open from 8:30 a.m. to 5 p.m. Monday through Friday, and from 11 a.m. to 4 p.m. on Saturday, customers are sure to find many unique items—each one hand-selected by Charles during his frequent buying excursions.

Although the inventory is always changing, constant staples of the store include Provencal commodes, Chinoiserie tables, Swedish-style armoires, and Staffordshire figurines. As a natural selection of Charles' design practice, the retail space is a celebration of contradiction. It is not uncommon to find Louis the XV Bergere chairs flanking a table made of sand and seashells. As Charles likes to say, "It's about the mix, not the match."

In addition to his design and retail work, Charles is actively involved in several charitable organizations. He is a founder of the Candlelight Home Tour, a board member of Tulsa Cares, past member of RAIN and St. Joseph Hospice, and is an active fundraiser for the Philbrook Museum of Art and the Cystic Fibrosis and Junior Diabetes Foundation.

❖

Charles Faudree.

CHARLES FAUDREE, INC.

PRUDENTIAL DETRICK REALTY

The company first opened as Hughes & Jones Realtors in February of 1938 at 408 Thompson Building in downtown Tulsa. Seth M. Hughes and Morgan Jones, the founders, were already well known in real estate in Tulsa, where they both graduated from Central High School in the 1920s. The Hughes family had originally settled in Tulsa in 1909 and the elder Hughes became the first cashier of the historic Exchange National Bank. Morgan moved with his family to Tulsa in 1917 and, after graduation, began a decade-long position with Adams and Leonard Realtors in the general brokerage of real estate. Morgan was also active in organizing the Tulsa Real Estate Salesman's Association. Succeeding his father in a successful mortgage loan company, Seth enjoyed a fine reputation as a builder and seller of homes across the city as he and Morgan joined forces to create the new realty company.

Although the name and location of the historic company has since changed, its founding principals and undisputed quality remain by providing clients in Tulsa and surrounding areas with excellent residential real estate services. The strong family support and traditions of Hughes and Jones are also reflected in the company as Sheldon 'Shel' Detrick, Jones' son-in-law became its CEO. Detrick entered the business in February 1960 after graduating from Oklahoma State University where he was later honored as a Distinguished Graduate. Jan

✧

Right: Seth Hughes (left) and Morgan Jones announced their new realtor organization in local newspapers on February 13, 1938.

Below: Sheldon Detrick and his daughter, Diana Detrick Medders, stand in a hallway gallery that tells the history of the company.

Jones Detrick, his wife of forty-four years, serves as corporate secretary/treasurer, and Diana Detrick Medders, Morgan Jones' granddaughter is vice president-technology.

Prudential Detrick Realty, as the company is known today, is headquartered at 4636 South Harvard Avenue in Tulsa; and the three Tulsa offices are part of a network of fourteen located in Oklahoma City, Albuquerque, New Mexico, and San Antonio, Texas. These offices have seventy plus employees, 700 plus Sales Associates, and last year closed over 6600 home sales at a value of over 800 million dollars.

Following in the traditions of its founders, the company remains involved in multiple aspects of civic, community and charitable activities, and is proud of its reputation for honesty, integrity, and customer service. Prudential Detrick Realty may be visited on the web at www.pruhomequest.com.

"Come stay where the warmth and friendliness is—just like home." Tucked away in the heart of east Tulsa, Lexington Hotel Suites allow guests easy access to all major highways, several area restaurants, shopping malls and is only six miles from Tulsa International Airport. Situated three miles from attractions like La Fortune Park and Golf Course and the IMAX Theater, Tulsa Lexington Suites has always appealed to business and leisure travelers alike. Within a ten-mile radius of the hotel, guests can visit favorite Tulsa attractions like the Performing Arts Center, The Gilcrease and The Philbrook Museums.

One of the rare amenities of Tulsa Lexington Suites is the benefit of being able to cook in the fully equipped kitchens. The guest rooms are thoughtfully equipped and feature an array of modern amenities such as a valet service, fitness facility privileges, meeting facilities, outdoor pool, wake up service, in-room coffee, alarm clock, voicemail, air conditioning, hair dryer, television and iron. The hotel staff is always friendly and warm, ready to meet the needs of every guest. Make one of Tulsa Lexington Suites' 162 room yours by calling 1-800-92-SUITE or take a drive to 8525 East Forty-first Street in Tulsa and see the hotel that promises the luxury of having your "Home away from home."®

✧

Above: Tulsa Lexington Suites include fully-equipped kitchens and comfortable living areas.

Bottom, left: A sparkling pool beckons hotel guests to enjoy a relaxing afternoon during their stay at Lexington Suites.

Bottom, right: Tulsa Lexington Suites is located along East Forty-first Street in Tulsa.

BRAZEAL MASONRY, INC.

Ron Brazeal knows the success that comes through dedication, education and hard work. Inspired by author Napoleon Hill, this native Tulsan founded Brazeal Masonry, Inc., in 1971, when he was only thirty years old.

Although his father was a plumber, Ron wanted to do something different. Working as a meat-cutter, he knew that someday he wanted to learn to lay brick. In 1963 he began an apprenticeship with Oklahoma Bricklayers and Allied Craftsman Local #9 Apprenticeship Training School. Southland Masonry Company provided on-the-job training under owner Smokey Howard. There, Ron learned such things as blueprint reading and how to manage a crew, all while completing his classroom studies.

As he gained expertise in the trade, Ron hired a Masontender and went to work doing small jobs until his experience in commercial masonry offered a natural transition into larger projects. The first large project was the Gatesway Foundation in Broken Arrow for Ray Conard Construction. Those larger jobs came gradually while developing business and management skills through night courses and daily experience. Ron set about hiring a full executive staff that included Don Pinkerton as director of field operation, Robert Conard as chief estimator, while Robert Bendabout, Art Brown, Raymond Cobler, Joe Murphy and Erling Overgaard served as job managers. The company continued to grow through the late 1970s and '80s and reached a high employment of 130 in the mid-1980s. Brazeal Masonry, Inc. developed a solid reputation for expertise and quality in the masonry industry. Ron reinvested profits in the company to provide growth and benefit the banking and bonding requirements.

✧

Above: Skyline Tower in Tulsa.

Below: St Paul United Methodist Church in Muskogee.

As Ron retired, Darren Brazeal became the company's president in 1994. This father-son team remained firm in their conviction that hiring the right people, letting them do their jobs, and rewarding them for a job well done is the key to Brazeal's continued success. Several employees have remained with the company over thirty years. Today the company employs between forty and seventy employees and most of their work has taken place in northeast Oklahoma with projects such as Skyline Tower, Woodland Hills Mall, and NSU in Broken Arrow, Tulsa Community College, Oral Roberts University and Tulsa University. As well as St. Francis and Tulsa Regional Medical Centers, Union, Jenks and Broken Arrow Public Schools, St. Paul United Methodist Church in Muskogee, Remington Park Grandstand in Oklahoma City, among many others.

Since 1971 the mission of Brazeal masonry has remained the same—to provide full service masonry construction and employ craftsmen who share in the company's belief that honesty, integrity, and skillful workmanship are the key ingredients for continued success in the industry. They are an equal opportunity employer and proudly support their community in projects for the United Way, Southeast Tulsa Jaycees, Living Arts of Tulsa, and the Tulsa Wheelmen Cycling Team.

Today ranked among the top 100 universities in the nation, The University of Tulsa traces its beginnings to Muskogee, Indian Territory, where the Presbyterian Church founded it in 1894 as a mission school for Indian girls.

From these pre-statehood roots grew Henry Kendall College, which was relocated to Tulsa in 1907 and re-chartered as The University of Tulsa (TU) in 1921.

The university's growing reputation for excellence reflects not only the vision of its pioneering benefactors, but also the talents of its students. In the fall of 2005, TU welcomed the most outstanding freshman class in university history, with a record number of National Merit Scholars (thirteen percent of the class) and nearly two-thirds of freshmen ranking in the top ten percent of their high school graduating classes. These high-achieving students from throughout the nation were attracted to Tulsa not only by TU's reputation, but also by its emphasis on personal attention: the average class size is nineteen and the student-to-faculty ratio is eleven to one.

In keeping with its core values, The University of Tulsa educates students for a rapidly changing and increasingly complex world. TU students come from forty-six states and sixty-one countries. A growing number of

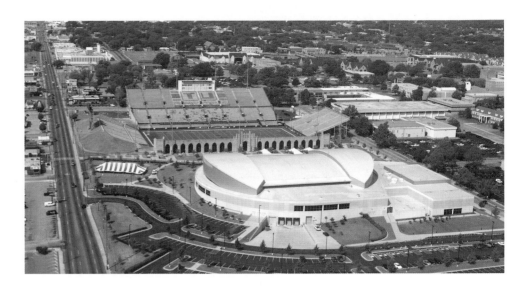

students live on the university's two-hundred-acre residential campus, which has expanded significantly over the past decade.

As a leading producer of experts and knowledge in a wide range of academic disciplines, The University of Tulsa has been internationally recognized for its petroleum-engineering program for more than half a century. Today this reputation also encompasses prominent programs in disciplines including computer science and Native American law.

The university also takes pride in its intercollegiate athletics program. The eighteen men and women's teams that comprise The University of Tulsa Golden Hurricane compete in the highest division of the NCAA. TU's recent entry into Conference USA has begun bringing new opponents and new exposure to the Golden Hurricane.

No profile of The University of Tulsa would be complete without mentioning the contributions of its graduates. TU is not simply an excellent school, but also an extended community. The university's growing alumni network includes chapters in ten cities: Chicago, Dallas, Denver, Fort Worth/Arlington, Houston, Kansas City, Oklahoma City, St. Louis, Tulsa, and Washington, D.C. This extended community of alumni brings recognition to TU across the nation, while providing the partnership and perspective that have advanced the university for more than one hundred years.

❖

Above: The University of Tulsa campus is located at 600 South College in Tulsa and on the internet at www.utulsa.edu.

Below: Students celebrate graduation at TU.

STEPHENSON OIL COMPANY

Joe Stephenson, Sr. fell in love with the bustling City of Tulsa during his summer breaks from high school in the early 1950s when he would come to visit his sister and work at the Ludwig Cigar Store located in the Phil Tower building, once home to Phillips Petroleum Company. Impressed with the oilmen that purchased high-dollar cigars in the store, Stephenson decided that he, too, would someday work for Phillips Petroleum.

The day after he graduated from Big Flat High School in Harriett, Arkansas in 1951, he packed his bags and headed for Tulsa where he worked as a welder for National Tank Company and as a route salesman for Meadow Gold before accepting a position in the sales department at Phillips Petroleum. In 1956 he was sent to change out a Phillips Service Station dealer in Stillwater…and ended up becoming that station's dealer.

It was here that he met his future wife, Betty. After they were married, they relocated to Oklahoma City and bought a Phillips Service Station on South Robinson. In 1958 the couple moved to Sand Springs and opened a Phillips Station as a consignor (a commissioned agent for Phillips) and bought their own franchise. From that point on, the business grew from 40,000 gallons per month to an average of 18 million gallons a year. Stephenson Oil Company anticipates a continued expansion of convenience stores and the addition of new wholesale customers over the next few years.

Stephenson Oil Company is now a three-part business that specializes in retail, wholesale and transport:

- JBJ Limited, d/b/a Stephenson Oil Company, is a wholesale gasoline business that specializes in petroleum marketing, selling gasoline to convenience stores as well as commercial accounts that include the local railroad company and area schools.

- Stephenson Oil Company d/b/a Joe's Gas and Grocery, a retail marketing business, consists of Citgo and Diamond Shamrock branded convenience stores, which are located throughout the Northeastern Oklahoma region. These operations are full-range convenience stores that sell Citgo and Diamond Shamrock products as well as groceries and delicatessen-style food, buffet pizza and Simple Simon Pizza.

- Stephenson Transport Incorporated delivers the fuel to Stephenson Oil Company convenience stores as well as other area retail and commercial accounts.

Each of the three business subgroups work dependently as the wholesale company sells fuel to the retail outlets that are delivered by the transport company.

Today the company employs approximately forty people with one employee who has worked for the company for over forty years. Joe D. Stephenson, Sr., serves as president; Betty Stephenson serves as secretary/treasurer; and their son, Joe D. Stephenson, Jr., serves as vice-president. All three have been involved in numerous community organizations, local and national charities over the years.

❖

Below: (From left to right) Joe, Betty, and Joe Stephenson, Sr., at the company headquarters on Charles Page Boulevard.

Bottom: One of the original Phillips Service Stations in Oklahoma located at 2800 South Robinson in Oklahoma City.

White Surveying Company is the oldest land surveying company in Oklahoma, providing land surveying and civil engineering services to Oklahoma and surrounding states for over sixty-six years.

Founded in the late 1930s by W. Kirk White as a side business during his tenure as a Registered Professional Engineer with the City of Tulsa Engineering Department. Kirk grew the business until his death in 1956, after which his family formed a partnership with Earl Denton. The company remained Denton & White Surveying Company until Earl's death in 1964. Lorraine White and David C. White established a partnership under the original company name, which was retained following Lorraine's death in 1975. David remains sole owner and continues to serve the company as CEO.

David White served as president of the Oklahoma Society of Land Surveyors (OSLS) and three years as a director of the American Congress on Surveying and Mapping (ACSM), and a Professional Engineer since 1968. David served on the City of Tulsa Board of Adjustment for ten years, with seven and a half years as chairman. He was also a member of the Tulsa Auxiliary Police (serving five years as director) and Tulsa Police Reserve for twenty years.

The president of White Surveying Company is Tom Haynes. Tom has been with the company since 1973 and has been a Registered Land Surveyor since 1978. He served as president of OSLS and is a member of ACSM.

Vice President Jim Smith has been with the company since 1977 and has been a Registered Land Surveyor since 1993. He also served as president of OSLS and is a member of ACSM.

Today, White Surveying Company provides a full range of land surveying services, including residential and commercial property transaction title surveys, ALTA/ACSM land title surveys, plot plans, mortgage inspection plats, boundary surveys, GPS surveys, elevation surveys, LOMA applications, and subdivision of land. Pioneering use of the most current technologies and techniques, combined with more than sixty-five years of archives, ensures the efficiency and accuracy of data collection

and plat generation. The company also partners with land surveying technology firms to test and improve their products.

As the company has grown from three to nearly thirty employees, including five Registered Land Surveyors and one Registered Professional Engineer, the mission of White Surveying Company remains the same: exceed the customer's expectations and provide exceptional surveying products that are prompt, clear, accurate, and competitively priced, in a professional and courteous manner. Every project receives thorough attention, benefiting from over 200 years of combined experience in land surveying and civil engineering. This standard of excellence has allowed White Surveying Company to

grow with its customers, maintaining strong business partnerships for over six decades.

White Surveying Company is located at 9936 East Fifty-Fifth Place in Tulsa, Oklahoma and on the Internet at www.whitesurveying.com.

WHITE SURVEYING COMPANY

✧

Below: White Surveying Company Office at 9936 East Fifty-Fifth Place in Tulsa, Oklahoma 74146.

Bottom: President Tom A. Haynes, Vice President Jim G. Smith, and Owner and CEO David C. White.

WAREHOUSE MARKETS, INC.

Clint V. Cox, Jr. was destined from birth to be a "grocery man." His grandfather and two uncles began the tradition by opening a general store in Hennessey shortly after the land run into Indian Territory. In the 1920's his father owned his own chain of stores in Arkansas before moving to Tulsa.

Clint Cox, Sr. borrowed $10,000 on his life insurance policy to open Warehouse Market at Tenth and Elgin, in what is considered one of Tulsa's most notable landmarks. The facade of the building, often referred to as the "Warehouse Market building" still stands as frontage for several new businesses.

When the first Warehouse Market store opened in July 1938, the depression was still on and grocery prices were low—Number two cans of tomatoes were five cents; Jell-O was three packages for thirteen cents; a ten pound bag of sugar cost forty-nine cents; Folger's Coffee was twenty-five cents; Vigo Dog Food sold for three cans at ten cents; and eggs were ten cents a dozen.

Warehouse Market sold only freshly dressed chickens. In those days, no one would buy a dead chicken. The customer would select the live chicken (kept in cages) and then a clerk would put a numbered metal tag around its neck and give the customer a slip of paper with the number on it. The customer would then continue shopping in the store while the chicken pickers would kill the chicken, dip it into a barrel of scalding water, and then pluck the feathers. This was all done in a location removed from the retail area, adjacent to the alley. A package boy would carry the dressed chicken on a tray to the retail meat department, where its number identified the chicken. The customer picked up her chicken at the retail meat counter. The package boy who had the job of carrying the freshly-dressed chicken or turkey from the backroom plucking area to the retail meat department eventually had a very bloody apron, so this job was not too desirable. The store had an especially large number of live turkeys that were caged in the basement during the Thanksgiving and Christmas holidays…you can imagine the mess!

Working beside his father over the years to build Warehouse Market, Clint, Jr. developed the common-sense attributes that have made the company the success it is today. He knew that operating a successful grocery business took more than just luck. He had the innate ability to determine when and where to open a new store, what type of product the customer was looking for and, more importantly, what price was fair for that product. He rewarded the hard work of his employees by promoting from within the company.

Warehouse Market was more than just a job for Clint. It was a lifetime endeavor to create a successful business to meet the needs of the community and provide jobs for hundreds of Oklahomans.

Because of his vision, today Warehouse Market operates sixteen supermarkets in Tulsa, Turley, Sand Springs, Broken Arrow, Sapulpa, Claremore, Okmulgee, and Oklahoma City, and includes over 1000 employees. It is still a family owned operation with two generations currently active in its operation.

When it was founded in 1918, Hillcrest Medical Center began as the vision of Dolly J. (Browne) McNulty to battle a growing influenza epidemic in the area. It was named Morningside Hospital & School of Nursing and was located in a small building at 521 North Boulder. The hospital became a not-for-profit organization in 1940 and developed into a large healthcare system in 1992.

In August 2004, Hillcrest HealthCare System (HHS) was purchased by Ardent Health Services, Nashville, Tennessee and is comprised of Hillcrest Medical Center, Tulsa Regional Medical Center (TRMC), Hillcrest Specialty Hospital, six regional hospitals, three medical residency training programs, and Utica Park Clinic/Hillcrest Medical Group, a primary care and specialty physician group with more than eighty-five physicians located across eastern Oklahoma.

Through its mission, HHS strives to be the leading provider of compassionate healthcare services for patients and their families, create a working environment of respect for every employee, physician and health professional, remain accountable for fiscal and ethical performances and establish a genuine responsibility to the communities it serves.

HHS offers the region's most comprehensive medical care in a variety of medical specialties and is a pioneer in providing new treatment options and the latest in technological advances in medicine. Whether it is being the only hospital in the state in 1949 to provide care to polio patients, to opening the Alexander Burn Center in 1968, one of only five facilities of its kind in the nation, to opening the region's

first dedicated women's hospital in 2003, HHS has remained at the forefront of outstanding comprehensive healthcare.

Since the founding of its initial facility, HHS has provided many "first-of-its-kind" procedures or facilities in Oklahoma—in 1957, the first closed heart surgery in Tulsa was performed at Hillcrest, followed by the area's first open heart surgery in 1962; the first kidney transplant in Tulsa was performed at Hillcrest in 1973; Oklahoma's first intraocular lens implant was performed at TRMC in 1974; the Leta M. Chapman Breast Health Center opened in 1996 and was Tulsa's first free standing facility dedicated to breast health. In 2001, Hillcrest Medical Center was the first hospital in Tulsa to offer intracoronary brachytherapy.

Hillcrest HealthCare System supports more than forty Tulsa community organizations. Through dozens of partnerships, sponsorships, fundraising projects, and mentoring and educational programs, HHS is uniquely positioned as a positive influence among every citizen of eastern Oklahoma, either directly or indirectly.

Through its community-based missions and vision of service, HHS continues to provide comprehensive healthcare services to Tulsa and surrounding areas. In partnership with its dedicated team of physicians, nurses, volunteers, administrative team members and leaders, HHS is committed to the health and wellness of the communities it serves.

For more information, visit the HHS website, www.hillcrest.com.

✧

Above: In 1927, Dolly McNulty, with the financial help of her husband, built Morningside Hospital, which later became Hillcrest Medical Center. The hospital is located at Twelfth and Utica.

Below: In the late 1950s, Hillcrest Medical Center dedicates a new wing of the hospital. The name changed from Hillcrest Morningside Hospital to Hillcrest Medical Center in 1952.

L.T. Mapping Services, Incorporated

It was a high school drafting class that helped Larry M. Tucker realize what he wanted to do in life. As Larry worked to perfect his drawing skills, judges at a regional contest awarded him first prize and set him on his way to a new career in drafting.

He moved to Tulsa in 1977 and worked for MAPCO before accepting a position at Jeffries and Associates. At both companies, Larry displayed outstanding managerial skills and was placed in supervisory positions. During his seventeen-year tenure as drafting supervisor at Jeffries, Larry worked on projects in thirty-six different states and transformed the drafting department from using hand-produced maps to creating computer-generated drawings—all before such technology became a standard element of the industry.

After Jeffries was sold, Larry worked with the new management team for about a year, then he and his wife Cheryl decided to start their own company. In 1997, L.T. Mapping Services, Inc. was born as three employees grew to six in the first year, and one client grew by two more by the second year. Within the next two years, the company included seventy-plus employees and numerous clients.

With the dot-com bust came a crash in the telecommunications industry. At one point, there were only four employees and for four months, Larry kept them employed out of loyalty. During this difficult time, the company had no income to speak of and Larry refused to take a salary, believing that his original employees had taken a chance on him when the company was founded, and that it was now his responsibility to return the favor.

Because of his strong business ethics and disciplined approach to financial management, the company was able to keep the original team through much of the recession. Sadly, nearly every competitor and many business associates had to close their doors.

However, as the telecommunications industry dwindles today, the oil and gas industry is growing and L.T. Mapping employs more than sixty employees again. Such success is due in no small part to the company's strong commitment to excellence and integrity while exceeding every client's expectations through the ongoing efforts of so many wonderful employees.

Cheryl continues in the company today as vice president in charge of human resources, financial planning, marketing, and office administration. Josh Thornbrugh, IT manager/GIS coordinator, manages the company network while developing and coordinating all GIS systems for the client base. He is also a member of the advisory board for Tri-County Technology in Bartlesville. Tracy Cowart, drafting supervisor/quality control, oversees all project schedules and maintains quality control assurance. Jim Edward is lead CAD technician and serves as project manager for several clients. Ian McCune, lead CAD technician, is a significant contributor on numerous pipeline and telecommunications projects directed by the company. Larry continues as the company's president and is honored to see so many of those he has mentored through the years succeed within the industry.

L.T. Mapping supports many charitable organizations including Red Maverick Scholarship Fund, Girl Scouts USA, The Pride of Bixby High School Band, Bixby Neighbors Food Bank, Oklahoma State Troopers, and Tulsa Fraternal Order of Police.

✧

Above: Larry Tucker taking care of business.

Below: Remaining members of the original staff: Cheryl Tucker, Larry Tucker, Tracy Cowart, Josh Thornbrugh, Ian McCune, and Jim Edwards.

UNDERCROFT
MONTESSORI
SCHOOL

When the Beatles first landed in America and Lyndon Johnson was elected the country's president, a group of Tulsa parents started a Montessori pre-school. They had read about Dr. Maria Montessori in Time magazine. The article outlined her extremely successful ways of teaching all children. If schools in other parts of the world and United States had Montessori schools for their children, then 1964 was certainly the time for a progressive Tulsa to have this special education available to any family.

Since that time Undercroft Montessori School has educated thousands of children ages three through fifteen from the Tulsa community. While the educational focus of this non-sectarian, nonprofit school centers around on the academic, physical, and emotional well being of the child, Undercroft serves parents and educators throughout the state and is known nationally as a resource for the Montessori educational philosophy.

In 1907, Dr. Maria Montessori, a visionary Italian anthropologist and Doctor of Medicine, who addressed the profound needs of the whole child, developed the "Montessori Method" of education. Under the direction of the specially trained Montessori teaching staff, the children of Undercroft Montessori School are offered a full range of academic and artistic programs along a developmental continuum.

The developmentally appropriate curriculum is designed to advance with the child and therefore creates a seamless education. The classrooms include self-selection of works by the student, use of compelling manipulative objects and careful observation and guidance by the teacher. Classes consist of multi-year age spans for social and intellectual collaboration and challenge. The classroom structure provides the ideal environment for the student's self-construction into adulthood.

With their love of learning, sophisticated skills in group work and firm academic grounding, Undercroft graduates move easily into surrounding schools.

Located at Thirty-sixth Place and Hudson Avenue, Undercroft Montessori School draws families of all backgrounds, from across Oklahoma, into a tight-knit community. This community both nurtures children and encourages their natural desire to "do it myself" in the very unique and always inspiring Montessori way. Exposure to the Montessori beliefs, which are firmly grounded in the principles of human development and to the school's supportive environment, dramatically enhances parenting skills.

Undercroft alumni are now leaders—well-known authors, artists, actors, business leaders and wonderful parents, who learned at the earliest age to believe in themselves and in education.

For more information about Undercroft, Tulsa's first Montessori school, please visit www.undercroft.org or call 918-622-2890 to arrange a tour of the campus.

✧

Above: Undercroft Montessori School today. The "little red schoolhouses" consist of four primary classrooms (shown) and a middle school building (not shown). A new elementrary building was opened in 1997.

Below: An early Undercroft graduation ceremony. Only one portion of the school's buildings was present and it was painted white. The early campus lacked many of the trees, which now provide extensive shade.

HALL, ESTILL, HARDWICK, GABLE, GOLDEN & NELSON, P.C.

For over forty years, Hall, Estill, Hardwick, Gable, Golden & Nelson, better know as Hall Estill, has offered a wide range of top notch legal services. Known for maintaining a focus on their client's needs, Hall Estill attorneys have provided expertise in virtually every area of the law and successfully assisted clients with matters in local, regional, national and international venues.

Established in 1966 as an oil and gas specialty practice, the firm was initially called Holloman, Hall & Abercrombie; becoming Hall & Estill in 1969. Their first large legal project was handling the acquisition of the Great Lakes Pipeline for the Williams Companies, who is still a client today. Founder Walter B. Hall continued his practice with the firm until his death in 1986.

The firm's capabilities grew as the clients' needs expanded. For example, in 1974 when one of their clients required legal expertise in labor and employment, the firm hired J. Patrick Cremin, to begin the practice group. Today, Cremin is still with Hall Estill and leads its largest practice group of ten attorneys.

The firm had several name changes in the 1970s as partners joined and left the group and settled in the mid-1980s on its current name, Hall, Estill, Hardwick, Gable, Golden & Nelson. Partner James C.T. Hardwick has been practicing law for more than forty years, much of the time with Hall Estill, and specializes in energy/natural resources and corporate law. Thomas D. Gable joined the firm in 1967 and maintains a practice in the fields of corporate, commercial and real estate law. Initially employed with Hall Estill as a summer clerk in 1968, Thomas F. Golden joined as an associate later that year and spent his career specializing in commercial law and legislative matters, as well as commercial real estate. He retired from the firm in 2003. Fred S. Nelson joined the firm in 1975 and maintained his practice there until he passed away in 1987.

Hall Estill's successful record of accomplishments range from persuading Circuit Court of Appeals to reverse prior published opinions to arguing cases before the U.S. Supreme Court. It now boasts more than one hundred practicing attorneys either in their Tulsa headquarters or at one of their three additional offices in Oklahoma City, northwest Arkansas and Washington, D.C.

This prestigious firm continues to provide its corporate clients with expert legal advice on all business-related matters, while at the same time ensuring that their individual clients receive personal attention for their estate, family and financial concerns. This integrated approach gives all clients a direct line to a team of preeminent legal practitioners brought together to address their specific needs. Headed by a lead attorney who functions as the client's personal representative and assembles an internal "legal partnership," this team will deliver the most current strategic counsel to resolve and economically manage any legal issues.

For more information about Hall Estill, visit them on the Internet at www.hallestill.com.

Above: (From left to right) Pamela H. Goldberg, Michael D. Cooke, James C. T. Hardwick, Andrew M. Wolov, Steven A. Broussard, Angelyn L. Dale, Robert F. Dougherty, and Betsy G. Jackson.

Below: Seated (from left to right): J. Kevin Hayes, James C. T. Hardwick, J. Patrick Cremin. Standing (from left to right): Michael D. Cooke, James D. Satrom, and Mark K. Blongewicz.

From nineteenth century mule-drawn wagons to twenty-first century big rigs, the Crace family knows transportation.

Jim Crace, co-founder of TruckStaff, LLC, learned everything he could about transportation as he listened to the legendary stories of his great-great grandfather, John Vaughan. A cowboy on the Chisholm Trail, Vaughan first bought a mule-team and wagon in the late 1860s in Oklahoma Territory. Carrying goods from Kansas and Missouri to Colorado and New Mexico, he met his future wife, Mary, in Colorado. She had three young daughters and accepted John's marriage proposal and the couple lived happily together until a disagreement erupted sometime in the 1880s. Mary loaded her children into a covered wagon and headed back to Oklahoma but John finally caught up with them near Erick. Mary refused to return to Colorado with him, saying he would have to bury her first. So that's exactly what John did—she was buried there in Erick fifty years later.

Settling in Erick, John turned to ranching as he transported cattle to markets across the country. When trucks began appearing around the country, they quickly became a necessity in the family business. Jim often says of his heritage, "We view the world from two perspectives—the seat of a horse or the seat of a truck."

As the Great Depression moved across America, John died and times were difficult in Erick. His son Richard moved to Sand Springs near the Osage Junction with its twenty acres of wooden pens—the largest shipping junction in the country. Richard settled in and was drafted into the military during World War II as a truck-driving instructor.

After Jim was born, Richard gave his grandson a hands-on education and had him driving trucks by the age of fifteen. Jim took a job pulling piggyback trailers off flat rail cars on weekends and, after graduation, went to work on the Katy Railroad while receiving his degree in business management. While working for Katy Railroad, Jim went to McAlester to off-load eighty cars of bombs and transport them to an ammunition plant–and landed himself a management

position because he was the only one who knew how to fill out the paperwork.

When Katy closed, Jim went to work as a driving instructor for Dick Lambert's Truck Driving School before becoming the Head of Safety and Driver Training for Penske Truck Leasing Company. His vast experience in the trucking field offered Jim the opportunity to own his own business and a battle with cancer nearly ended that dream in 1997. But a chance introduction to Mike Morrison—a transplanted Tulsan, former architect, and astute businessman—changed everything.

Mike and Jim agreed that TruckStaff was born out of necessity simply because, until its creation, truck drivers had few of the basic skills necessary for an often-difficult job. Their idea was a success and today TruckStaff employs between 150 and 250 drivers to corporate businesses nationwide, while offering problem-solving skills for improving systems to use their highly trained and experienced drivers. In the next ten years, ten new offices are planned nationwide.

Today, Jim leads safety seminars nationwide as part of the Homeland Security Department's National Highway Watch Program and is Chairman for the Oklahoma Safety Management Council of the Oklahoma Trucking Association.

Successful and dedicated family men, Jim says "life is about experience" while Mike believes that Jim's greatest success, both in business and health, is his endless, positive outlook.

TRUCKSTAFF, LLC

✧

Below: Jim Crace with the next generation—Coy is on horse and Cale is in the stroller.

Bottom: John Vaughn stands amid a wool train leaving Taos Plaza, c. 1904.

MCLEMORE INSURANCE AGENCY INCORPORATED

✧

Above: McLemore Insurance Agency was originally founded before statehood, in 1903.

Below: McLemore Insurance.

McLemore Insurance Agency has been serving the commercial and personal property and casualty insurance needs of area customers and businesses for well over a century. This historic agency was founded by M.D. Rhodes in 1903 and counted among its original policyholders two of Tulsa's three doctors as well as a number of oil company operators. Thomas Anderson purchased the agency around the end of World War I and sold it to his son, Loyd, in the mid-1930s. Over the next twenty years, the agency continued to grow and prosper along with the city.

In 1954, John McLemore, Jr., at the time a special agent with Kemper Insurance, became interested in buying the agency. Anderson must have seen John's bankbook because the purchase took every cent he had to his name. After pleading with a man to sell him a car with no money down and twelve installments, John became the proud owner of the agency on August 1, 1954.

John's desire to deal fairly and honestly with customers and companies has remained the underlying foundation for the business' continued success into the twenty-first century. For many years, John was a member of the State Board of Directors for Professional Insurance Agents and served as the group's president in 1971. He was also a member on its National Board for five years. John III served on the Local Independent Agents of Greater Tulsa for ten years as a board member and was president in 1996. Among his family and friends, John, Jr. is also well remembered for his brush with stardom during the filming of the epic movie *Tulsa*, which opened in theatres in 1949, when he served as Oscar winner Susan Hayward's bodyguard!

The agency's famous connections have certainly continued throughout the years as many interesting individuals and companies have sought the expertise of the outstanding agents of McLemore Insurance. Such figures as former Harlem Globetrotter Marcus Haynes, singer/musician Steve Ripley, Oscar-winning actress Shirley MacLaine, and the father of former Oklahoma Governor Frank Keating have all experienced the fine service that has characterized McLemore Insurance from the very beginning. The company's rich heritage has brought many famous doctors, lawyers, politicians, and businessmen—all among the best personal customers an agent or company could wish for.

John's son, John T. McLemore III joined his father in the agency in 1984, became its owner and president in 1995, and has continued the stable growth that his father so carefully established a half-century before. Serving customer needs through loss control, loss prevention and insurance, today the agency employs fifteen staff members and agents and totals $8 million in sales and $1 million in revenue. The agency also celebrated the grand opening of its new headquarters at 6965 South Sixty-Ninth East Avenue in Tulsa, and plans are underway to merge in other agencies and expand the company's non-standard auto agency (AIM) into several new satellite locations.

John III and his wife Chris, who has worked in the agency for seventeen years, see a bright future for the historic agency and looks forward to many years in the market for small-to medium-sized commercial accounts and personal lines business. John credits longtime employee Sue Jackson with one of his favorite bits of wisdom in the business—"every file has an interesting story." Knowing the customers, not just their policies, has been the secret for longevity in the insurance business.

Being a good agent, a good employer and a good industry and civic citizen—those are the things that have made McLemore Insurance Agency one of Tulsa's most historic businesses.

For more information about McLemore Insurance, visit www.mclemoreinsurance.com.

Before 1970, people in Tulsa and the surrounding areas who wanted to attend college had few choices unless they were willing to travel to Stillwater, Norman, Tahlequah, or attend private college. It was out of this need that Tulsa Community College was born. Oklahomans organized and lobbied the state legislature for a junior college to be established in the city and, in April 1969, Resolution 517 established what was then called Tulsa Junior College (TJC), with Dr. Alfred M. Philips as its first president. Dr. Dean P. VanTrease soon joined the staff as executive vice-president, along with several other staff and faculty who later became known as "TJC Originals." When the new school opened its doors in September 1970 the main "campus" consisted of leased space on the first three floors of the Sinclair Oil Building at 909 South Boston. In 1989, Dr. Philips retired and Dr. VanTrease became president. He served in that capacity until his retirement in June 2004 whereupon Dr. Thomas K. McKeon became TCC's current president.

In May 1996 the Oklahoma legislature approved a resolution by the school's Board of Regents to change the name of Tulsa Junior College to Tulsa Community College (TCC). Supporters believed that the name change was necessary because "TCC is, and always has been, a 'community college' and that college name should reflect the institution's unique identity and place in the greater metropolitan area."

Since its inception, the college has remained committed to excellence in instruction, student services, and programs relevant to the needs and interests of the greater Tulsa area. Believing in the growth and worth of the person as an individual and as a member of society, the College offers credit, transfer, and workforce development and continuing education programs.

Statistically, TCC is nearly unmatched in its student growth. Enrollment reached 2,796 students in the first year; approximately 425,000 people have attended classes in the last 35 years. By 1974 the original leased structure was purchased and remodeled to become the Metro Campus. Construction for the Northeast Campus began in the Spring of 1978, and the campus was opened in January 1979. Development of the Southeastern Campus began in 1981, and it opened in 1984. In April 1990 the Board of Regents approved a land gift of eighty acres from Tulsan Stephen Jatras. That site became Tulsa Junior College West Campus, opening in 1996. The school currently employs 2,885 full-time, part-time and adjunct faculty and staff members and serves 27,000 different students in college credit classes annually.

In the twenty-first century, Tulsa Community College continues to provide and significantly enhance access to high quality, affordable education and student support services. For more information about the exciting events taking place at TCC or to enroll in the upcoming semester of available courses, call (918) 595-7000 or visit them on the web at www.tulsacc.edu.

TULSA COMMUNITY COLLEGE

❖

Above: The Metro Campus Student Union at Tulsa Community College

Below: The Math and Science Building is located on the Southeast campus of Tulsa Community College.

VINTAGE PETROLEUM, INCORPORATED

Born in the oil and gas fields of Oklahoma in 1983, Vintage Petroleum, Incorporated, grew rapidly into a global, independent energy company engaged in the acquisition, exploitation and exploration of oil and gas properties and the marketing of crude oil and natural gas. It was listed on the New York Stock Exchange in 1990.

Since the company's founding, Vintage focused on extracting the maximum amount of value from producing oil and natural gas assets. Vintage did this by acquiring producing properties with significant upside potential at competitive costs. Then, through development activities, the Vintage team unlocked the upside potential of acquired properties, increasing production and adding reserves. Vintage also explored for oil and natural gas through a balanced risk program designed to grow reserves and production in the United States in the near term, and through a potentially high-impact program targeting areas outside the company's core operations with a longer-term time frame. This strategy led Vintage to dramatic increases in production and reserves. All the while, Vintage increased its capabilities from both a technological standpoint and from a geographical-reach standpoint. All of these factors led to Vintage's impressive operating and financial results over its twenty-two-year history.

The cornerstone of the company, its producing property base in the United States, was built through a series of acquisitions during a period when the major oil companies were divesting their domestic properties in favor of growing their international asset base. Domestic operations focused on the West Coast, Gulf Coast, East Texas, and Mid-Continent areas of the country. Exploiting these assets, while exploring for new oil and gas reserves, provided Vintage with a management and technical base to begin building a global portfolio in the mid-1990s.

In 1995, Vintage took its proven business model honed in the U.S. and expanded its operations into Argentina, with entry into Bolivia following soon thereafter. By establishing local offices with experienced staff in each of these areas, and by utilizing the latest exploration and development technology such as three-dimensional seismic surveying, Vintage profitably built its reserve and production base in South America.

Vintage's frontier exploration program also led the company halfway around the world in 1999 to the middle eastern Republic of Yemen, where initial drilling success warranted the building of a permanent pipeline and processing facility in the area.

By 2004, Vintage had accumulated an interest in more than 4,800 wells and revenues had risen to $778 million. Vintage's estimated proved reserves at year-end 2004, were 437.2 million barrels of oil equivalent, composed of 297 million barrels of oil accounting for 68 percent of total reserves and 840 billion cubic feet of natural gas accounting for the remaining 32 percent of proved reserves.

Application of Vintage's historical strategy of acquire, exploit and explore, coupled with high energy prices, brought about robust operational and financial success for the company in 2005. With renewed acquisition activity, a strong balance sheet, and rising production in all of its operating areas, Vintage's stock price outperformed traditional market indices and that of many of its industry peers. Vintage's success did not go unnoticed during this time of industry consolidation, and in early 2006 Vintage successfully capped its twenty-two-year history by merging with Occidental Petroleum.

But Vintage was not just about oil and gas. Through its operating experience worldwide, Vintage recognized that it must be cognizant of the people, communities, and cultures in which it operated, of its responsibility to the environment, and the role each plays in creating shareholder value. Vintage was committed to all the communities in which it operated, and actively supported various charitable and educational organizations, as well as employee volunteerism. As visible leaders of this commitment, Vintage Petroleum's co-founder Charles C. Stephenson, Jr. and his wife Peggy continue to be active participants in and supporters of numerous local, state and national charities.

✧

Charles C. Stephenson, Jr.

Holland Hall is an independent, coeducational, college preparatory Episcopal affiliated day school offering classes for students from Preschool through twelfth grade. As a premier college preparatory institution, Holland Hall provides students with exceptional academic, arts, and athletic opportunities.

Miss Winnifred Schureman, the school's first headmistress, was recruited from her position as a camp director in Minnesota by a group of ten prominent Tulsa men who were concerned about their children's educational preparation for admission into eastern colleges. The school was given the name Holland Hall as a tribute to Miss Schureman's Dutch ancestry.

Holland Hall occupies 162 acres in South Tulsa, near Eighty-First Street between Sheridan and Yale. When the school opened September 21, 1922, Holland Hall was located in a rented building at 909 South Cheyenne. That building is no longer standing, but the legacy of that first vision proudly continues today. Chartered in 1930, Holland Hall has grown from sixty students and eight teachers to over 1,025 students and 200 faculty and staff members. Although the original building was quickly outgrown, facilities on five different campuses were utilized before moving to its permanent home.

In 1970 the campus was moved to the current location with the opening of the Upper School. The Primary School was added in 1976 and the Middle School in 1982, uniting the whole school on a single campus. Additional facilities, including the Walter Arts Center (1992) and the Outdoor Sports Complex, including the Charles H. Brown Football Field (1995) have provided outstanding resources to generations of students. The most recent addition to the campus, which opened in 2000, is the Duenner Family Science, Math and Technology Center. The school, which now graduates more students in a single class, than were graduated in its first ten years, has more than 2,800 alumni around the world.

For more information, contact Holland Hall at 918-481-1111 or visit their website at www.hollandhall.org.

✧

Above: In its more than eighty years of existence, Holland Hall has had a rich history and sense of tradition. This plaque has traveled from campus to campus since 1936. It currently greets visitors to the campus, along with a statue representing the purpose of the school "a community that educates, nurtures and empowers the individual student for lifelong learning."

Below: Holland Hall's home from 1938-1970. The building at 2640 South Birmingham Place is perhaps one of the most recognized former locations of the school. Facilities at the Birmingham location developed over the years, gradually increasing the campus to include more than eleven buildings and support structures before all three schools were combined in 1982 on the current campus on Eighty-First Street.

UNLAUB COMPANY

The Unlaub Company provides power transmission and material handling products and services, including electric motors, v-belts and synchronous belts, pulleys and sheaves; bearings, couplings and bushings; conveyor belting and other conveyor components; plus many other related products and a service team to provide installation, lubrication, inspection and custom tailored services. Unlaub serves many industries in the region including oil and gas, aggregate, agricultural, food processing, original equipment manufacturers and a wide range of other companies, large and small.

After years of experience selling v-belts and related products, C. G. (Charles Griswald) Unlaub started the Unlaub Company in 1948 at 1722 East King Place in Tulsa. In 1953, Bob Coulter joined Unlaub after serving in the Korean War. When Unlaub died in 1979, Coulter bought a controlling interest in Unlaub. "BJ" and his wife, Billie, survived the economic downturn in the 1980s and directed Unlaub into a stable, customer focused company. Through the 1990s, two of their four children, Karen and Rod, assumed an operational role in the company. Today, Rod Coulter leads the company of sixteen employees, continually expanding product and service offerings, as well as enhancing Unlaub's tradition of excellent customer service. Customers in Oklahoma, Kansas, and Arkansas are still served by the original location.

❖

Above: The Unlaub Company office/warehouse has been at the same location since 1948.

Below: Rod Coulter grew up with the Unlaub Company. He was well trained by his Dad and sister and now leads the company.

The Unlaub business plan is essentially to serve the customer with the products, services and support that they need to stay competitive and thriving in their respective industries. Unlaub will continue to expand its product line and experience to meet the needs of their customers. A solid focus on customer service has been the primary reason for Unlaub's success and longevity over the years. As they move into the new millennium, an important goal of the company is to protect and expand the customer base using newer technologies where appropriate but also maintaining and developing the fundamental, unchanging requirements of building solid customer relationships and delivering exceptional customer service. Unlaub believes that this basic goal, coupled with a commitment to the highest ideals and ethics of a business enterprise are the foundation of Unlaub's future success. Upon this foundation, they intend to expand their core product/service lines, develop new product lines, as well as the knowledge and tools necessary to make Unlaub one of the very finest places to work and do business in Tulsa and Northeastern Oklahoma.

Making a difference in the Tulsa community since 1948, the Unlaub Company is a proud supporter of the Tulsa Boy's Home and Coulter has served on the Tulsa Boy's Home Board of Directors. Coulter believes "it is vital that Unlaub return to the citizens of its sales area a portion of its profits so that both the company and the people of Oklahoma benefit from its success."

Michael McDaniel and Scott Webb began talking about the dream of opening their own engineering firm while working at an international architectural engineering company in Tulsa. After establishing a number of solid relationships with local architectural firms, the pair proudly announced the opening of McDaniel-Webb Design Group LLC on April 15, 1997. They each contributed fifty dollars to the venture and have never borrowed a dime of capital since. The company was reorganized in February of the next year and welcomed Gregory Patovisti as an equal partner under their new name—MPW Engineering.

From the beginning the company gained in-depth expertise for developing design standards and criteria for building owners. In 1999 the firm's work on single building projects gave way to maintaining prototypical construction detail libraries for major retail companies. The firm began producing full design fire protection construction documents in 2004, a key addition to the types of engineering services offered today. Steady growth has allowed MPW Engineering to expand into the production of mechanical, electrical, plumbing, and fire protection construction documents—engineering the very places where people live, work, shop, play, dine, learn, and heal.

The reputation and success of MPW depends greatly upon and thrives due to the experience, quality, and dedication of its employees. The firm constantly searches for people who have the skills and traits that are required to provide the level of service that MPW's clients expect and the company demands.

MPW Engineering's mission is to "Make It Happen," and through their combined expertise, knowledge and experience the firm knows well the demands of clients and what it takes to offer them a successful project. They are well-regarded for going the extra mile to meet deadlines and produce high quality work that is outstanding in appearance, consistency and format, and they take great pride in being

MPW ENGINEERING

able to adapt to their client's exacting standards. Located in downtown Tulsa, the company is honored by the success that has transformed Mike, Greg and Scott's dream into a reality. Through hard work and determination, they made it happen.

Discover more about the company at www.mpwengineering.com.

❖

Above: The principals of MPW Engineering are (from left to right) Michael D. McDaniel, Gregory A. Patovisti, and Scott C. Webb.

Below: One of MPW's first projects: Holy Family Cathedral School Renovation in 1997.

BARRON & HART

Born in Shawnee in 1919, M. I. Barron understood loss and tragedy at a young age. While living in Kaw City, his family barely survived a devastating flood before moving to Enid. Though he suffered a hearing loss as a child, he dreamed of being a Music Minister and attended Southwest Bible School until a spiraling economy forced him to leave. His hearing loss kept him from serving in World War II, but Barron found success when he joined the Corps of Engineers, married his long time sweetheart Opal and moved to Kansas before being transferred to Tulsa. While with the Corps he proudly worked on a new project, the Kaw City Dam, which was specifically designed to prevent floods like the one suffered by his own family when he was just a boy.

to attract customers, but Barron and Hart did make it—right into the twenty-first century—by always offering the same high quality service in an excellent work environment.

Barron's oldest son Barry worked in Tulsa for City Service Occidental for thirty years before accepting a position with the Williams companies, while his youngest son Bryon, who joined the family business as an expert car washer at the age of six, leads Barron and Hart today.

Much has changed since 1947. In the 1960s Dupont sent sales reps to Barron for training in the use of their products. Now Bryon sends his employees to seminars throughout the country to keep them up-to-date on rapid industry changes. One of those changes involves learning how to work on electric cars, which are predicted to corner twenty percent of the market in about five years.

But with all of the changes that technology and time have brought to Barron and Hart, their foundational principles and outstanding workmanship remain unchanged. Bryon maintains the strong work ethic and integrity instilled in him by his father and meets the challenges of today's work place with courage and capability, and values the importance of long time employees and customers.

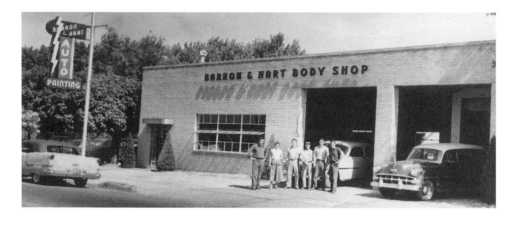

❖

Top, right: M. I. Barron, founder of Barron and Hart.

Above: The Barron and Hart team, c. the 1950s.

Below: A Barron and Hart postcard, c. the 1950s.

As the war and his work with the Corps of Engineers ended, Barron dreamed of doing what he loved best—restoring cars. He worked for a while for another man and then in 1947 bought a piece of property at 2909 East Fifteenth Street and began his own business. Most people said he would never make it because the place was too far out in the country

Creating a positive experience for our clients and providing quality aircraft that matches each customer's specific needs has long been the guiding principle of Dan W. Howard and the staff of Dan Howard Aircraft Sales.

Founded as a one-man operation from his home on April 7, 1999, Dan entered the industry with a proven background in the field–first as a retired state trooper pilot for the Oklahoma Highway Patrol and then as an airline pilot.

Today, the company is among the top purveyors of quality high-performance aircraft in the country and sells more Cessna 210 Centurion aircraft than any other dealer in the world. In 2001, Dan moved the business to Bill Christiansen's Jet Center at Richard L. Jones, Jr.

"Riverside" Airport. Annual sales exceed $10 million and the company serves an international customer base. Plans for future growth include development of a Cessna Citation Jet brokerage and management department to better serve Tulsa's growing need for personal and corporate jet transportation.

Dan's son, Colt Howard, has recently joined the firm in a part-time entry-level position and Dan looks forward to his growing participation in the business over the years to come. Another member of the team, Robert Parenti, now serves as sales manager. His advice and counsel in key company decisions are highly regarded.

Dan Howard Aircraft Sales, Inc. is located at 200 West Learjet Lane in Tulsa and on the

DAN HOWARD AIRCRAFT SALES, INCORPORATED

INDEX

SPONSORS

ABOUT THE AUTHORS

BERYL FORD was born in Tulsa and has worked for decades as a builder and structural inspector. Along the way, he amassed a collection of nearly 250,000 photographs and historical artifacts of Tulsa County. As the county's most noted historian, he has served as president of the Tulsa Pioneers Association and twice as president of the Tulsa County Historical Society. He and his wife, Lydia, have six children—Russell, Robert, Richard, Ronald, Ross, and Annette. He is a member of the Tulsa Central High School Hall of Fame and was a founder of the Tulsa Air and Space Museum. In 2004, he was named "Tulsan of the Year" by *TulsaPeople* magazine.

CHARLES FORD, Beryl's younger brother, is a real estate investment broker with a long history of public service and interest in history and the arts. Born in Tulsa, he served in the Oklahoma legislature from 1966 to 2004. He was the senior member of the state legislature upon his retirement. In the past decade, he has spearheaded efforts to display permanent fine art in the halls of the legislature in the State Capitol. A member of the Tulsa Central High School Hall of Fame, Ford and his wife, Pat, have four children, Christopher, Roger, Karin, and Robyn.

RODGER RANDLE is a former mayor of Tulsa and president pro tempore of the Oklahoma State Senate. He was born in Tulsa and attended Will Rogers High School, the University of Oklahoma, and the University of Tulsa School of Law. After serving as mayor, he became president of Rogers State University. He now lives in Tulsa with his wife, Judy, and teaches at the University of Oklahoma Tulsa campus.

BOB BURKE, a native of Broken Bow, Oklahoma, has written more historical biographies (30) than anyone else in American history and more books about Oklahoma (60) than anyone else. He is a graduate of the University of Oklahoma and the Oklahoma City University School of Law. He was director of a large state agency in the administration of Governor David Boren and managed Boren's first race for the United States Senate in 1978. He and his wife, Chimene, live in Oklahoma City where he practices law and writes books. He is the father of Robert, Amy, and Cody and step father of Natalie, Lauren, and Calli.

ABOUT THE COVER

Friends For a Day, an oil painting by Wayne Cooper, depicts the brief friendship of Count Albert-Alexandre de Porutales, a twenty-one-year-old member of Washington Irving's party, and a young Osage boy who brought a stray horse into Irving's camp on his visit to Tulsa County in 1832. The Cherokees believed the horse was stolen and ordered the boy flogged. However, Irving's men rescued him and Porutales made the lad his personal squire. In the painting, the Osage boy and Porutales are scouting the countryside on Bald Hill, northeast of present-day Sand Springs. The rock marks an Osage hunting trail.

COURTESY OF THE OKLAHOMA STATE SENATE HISTORICAL PRESERVATION FUND, INC.

For more information about the following publications or about publishing your own book, please call
Historical Publishing Network at 800-749-9790 or visit www.lammertinc.com.

Black Gold: The Story of Texas Oil & Gas
Historic Abilene: An Illustrated History
Historic Amarillo: An Illustrated History
Historic Anchorage: An Illustrated History
Historic Austin: An Illustrated History
Historic Beaufort County: An Illustrated History
Historic Beaumont: An Illustrated History
Historic Bexar County: An Illustrated History
Historic Brazoria County: An Illustrated History
Historic Charlotte: An Illustrated History of Charlotte and Mecklenburg County
Historic Cheyenne: A History of the Magic City
Historic Comal County: An Illustrated History
Historic Corpus Christi: An Illustrated History
Historic Denton County: An Illustrated History
Historic Edmond: An Illustrated History
Historic El Paso: An Illustrated History
Historic Erie County: An Illustrated History
Historic Fairbanks: An Illustrated History
Historic Gainesville & Hall County: An Illustrated History
Historic Henry County: An Illustrated History
Historic Houston: An Illustrated History
Historic Illinois: An Illustrated History
Historic Kern County: An Illustrated History of Bakersfield and Kern County
Historic Laredo: An Illustrated History of Laredo & Webb County
Historic Louisiana: An Illustrated History
Historic Midland: An Illustrated History
Historic Montgomery County: An Illustrated History of Montgomery County, Texas
Historic Oklahoma: An Illustrated History
Historic Oklahoma County: An Illustrated History
Historic Omaha: An Illustrated History of Omaha and Douglas County
Historic Pasadena: An Illustrated History
Historic Passaic County: An Illustrated History
Historic Philadelphia: An Illustrated History
Historic Prescott: An Illustrated History of Prescott & Yavapai County
Historic Richardson: An Illustrated History
Historic Rio Grande Valley: An Illustrated History
Historic Scottsdale: A Life from the Land
Historic Shreveport-Bossier: An Illustrated History of Shreveport & Bossier City
Historic Texas: An Illustrated History
Historic Victoria: An Illustrated History
Historic Williamson County: An Illustrated History
Iron, Wood & Water: An Illustrated History of Lake Oswego
Miami's Historic Neighborhoods: A History of Community
Old Orange County Courthouse: A Centennial History
Plano: An Illustrated Chronicle
The New Frontier: A Contemporary History of Fort Worth & Tarrant County
The San Gabriel Valley: A 21st Century Portrait